God's Promises®
for
Fathers

God's Promises®
for
Fathers

Published by
THOMAS NELSON
Since 1798
www.thomasnelson.com

Published in Nashville, Tennessee by Thomas Nelson, Inc.

Thomas Nelson, Inc. titles may be purchased in bulk for educational, business, fund-raising, or sales promotional use. For information, please e-mail SpecialMarkets@ThomasNelson.com.

Cover design by Greg Jackson, ThinkPen Design.

ISBN-10: 1-4041-1328-2 (NKJV)
ISBN-13: 978-1-4041-1328-2 (NKJV)
ISBN-10: 1-4041-1343-6 (SS)
ISBN-13: 978-1-4041-1343-5 (SS)

Printed in the United States of America

07 08 09 10 11 BANTA 9 8 7 6 5 4 3 2 1

Contents

God Freely Gives You

God Asks You To

God Gives You Strength When

God Protects You When

God Challenges You To

God Listens To Your Prayers When

God Fills You With Joy When

God Keeps You Secure When

God Comforts You When

God's Special Love Is With You When

God Shares Your Dreams For

God Rejoices When

God's Dynamic Examples
Of Fathers Who Cared

GOD FREELY
GIVES YOU

Eternal hope for your family

∞

Sing to the LORD with thanksgiving;
Sing praises on the harp to our God,
Who covers the heavens with clouds,
Who prepares rain for the earth,
Who makes grass to grow on the mountains.
He gives to the beast its food,
And to the young ravens that cry.
He does not delight in the strength of the horse;
He takes no pleasure in the legs of a man.
The LORD takes pleasure in those who fear Him,
In those who hope in His mercy.
Praise the LORD, O Jerusalem!
Praise your God, O Zion!
For He has strengthened the bars of your gates;
He has blessed your children within you.

Psalm 147:7–13

But let us who are of the day be sober, putting on the breastplate of faith and love, and as a helmet the hope of salvation.

For God did not appoint us to wrath, but to obtain salvation through our Lord Jesus Christ, who died for us, that whether we wake or sleep, we should live together with Him.

Therefore comfort each other and edify one another, just as you also are doing.

I Thessalonians 5:8–11

But God, who is rich in mercy, because of His great love with which He loved us,

even when we were dead in trespasses, made us alive together with Christ (by grace you have been saved),

and raised us up together, and made us sit together in the heavenly places in Christ Jesus,

That in the ages to come He might show the exceeding riches of His grace in His kindness toward us in Christ Jesus.

Ephesians 2:4–7

If then you were raised with Christ, seek those things which are above, where Christ is, sitting at the right hand of God.

Set your mind on things above, not on things on the earth.

For you died, and your life is hidden with Christ in God.

When Christ who is our life appears, then you also will appear with Him in glory.

Colossians 3:1–4

Because of the hope which is laid up for you in heaven, of which you heard before in the word of the truth of the gospel,

which has come to you, as it has also in all the world, and is bringing forth fruit, as it is also among you since the day you heard and knew the grace of God in truth.

Colossians 1:5–6

Knowing that a man is not justified by the works of the law but by faith in Jesus Christ, even we have believed in Christ Jesus, that we might be justified by faith in Christ and not by the works of the law; for by the works of the law no flesh shall be justified.

I have been crucified with Christ; it is no longer I who live, but Christ lives in me; and the life which I now live in the flesh I live by faith in the Son of God, who loved me and gave Himself for me.

Galatians 2:16, 20

Therefore let that abide in you which you heard from the beginning. If what you heard from the beginning abides in you, you also will abide in the Son and in the Father.

And this is the promise that He has promised us—eternal life.

I John 2:24–25

For the wages of sin is death, but the gift of God is eternal life in Christ Jesus our Lord.

Romans 6:23

For as many as are led by the Spirit of God, these are sons of God.

For you did not receive the spirit of bondage again to fear, but you received the Spirit of adoption by whom we cry out, "Abba, Father."

The Spirit Himself bears witness with our spirit that we are children of God,

and if children, then heirs—heirs of God and joint heirs with Christ, if indeed we suffer with Him, that we may also be glorified together.

For I consider that the sufferings of this present time are not worthy to be compared with the glory which shall be revealed in us.

For we were saved in this hope, but hope that is seen is not hope; for why does one still hope for what he sees?

But if we hope for what we do not see, we eagerly wait for it with perseverance.

Romans 8:14–18, 24–25

Blessed be the God and Father of our Lord Jesus Christ, who according to His abundant mercy has begotten us again to a living hope through the resurrection of Jesus Christ from the dead, to an inheritance incorruptible and undefiled and that does not fade away, reserved in heaven for you,

who are kept by the power of God through faith for salvation ready to be revealed in the last time.

In this you greatly rejoice, though now for a little while, if need be, you have been grieved by various trials,

that the genuineness of your faith, being much more precious than gold that perishes, though it is tested by fire, may be found to praise, honor, and glory at the revelation of Jesus Christ,

whom having not seen you love. Though now you do not see Him, yet believing, you rejoice with joy inexpressible and full of glory,

receiving the end of your faith—the salvation of your souls.

I Peter 1:3–9

I have fought the good fight, I have finished the race, I have kept the faith.

Finally, there is laid up for me the crown of righteousness, which the Lord, the righteous Judge, will give to me on that Day, and not to me only but also to all who have loved His appearing.

II Timothy 4:7–8

The wisdom you seek
for your children
∞

My son, pay attention to my wisdom;
Lend your ear to my understanding,
That you may preserve discretion,
And your lips may keep knowledge.

Proverbs 5:1–2

The fear of the LORD is the beginning of wisdom;
A good understanding have all those who do His
commandments.
His praise endures forever.

Psalm 111:10

The days of our lives are seventy years;
And if by reason of strength they are eighty years,
Yet their boast *is* only labor and sorrow;
For it is soon cut off, and we fly away.
Who knows the power of Your anger?
For as the fear of You, so is Your wrath.
So teach us to number our days,
That we may gain a heart of wisdom.

Psalm 90:10–12

Oh, how I love Your law!
It is my meditation all the day.
You, through Your commandments, make me
wiser than my enemies;
For they are ever with me.
I have more understanding than all my teachers,
For Your testimonies are my meditation.
I understand more than the ancients,
Because I keep Your precepts.
I have restrained my feet from every evil way,
That I may keep Your word.
I have not departed from Your judgments,
For You Yourself have taught me.
How sweet are Your words to my taste,
Sweeter than honey to my mouth!
Through Your precepts I get understanding;
Therefore I hate every false way.

Psalm 119:97–104

"Get wisdom! Get understanding!
Do not forget, nor turn away from the words of
my mouth.
Do not forsake her, and she will preserve you;
Love her, and she will keep you.
Wisdom is the principal thing;
Therefore get wisdom. And in all your getting,
get understanding.

Exalt her, and she will promote you;
She will bring you honor, when you embrace her.
She will place on your head an ornament of
grace;
A crown of glory she will deliver to you."
Hear, my son, and receive my sayings,
And the years of your life will be many.
I have taught you in the way of wisdom;
I have led you in right paths.

Proverbs 4:5–11

How much better to get wisdom than gold!
And to get understanding is to be chosen rather than
silver.

Proverbs 16:16

Happy is the man who finds wisdom,
And the man who gains understanding;
For her proceeds are better than the profits of silver,
And her gain than fine gold.
She is more precious than rubies,
And all the things you may desire cannot compare
with her.
Length of days is in her right hand,
In her left hand riches and honor.
Her ways are ways of pleasantness,
And all her paths are peace.

She is a tree of life to those who take hold of her,
And happy are all who retain her.
The LORD by wisdom founded the earth;
By understanding He established the heavens;
By His knowledge the depths were broken up,
And clouds drop down the dew.
My son, let them not depart from your eyes—
Keep sound wisdom and discretion;
So they will be life to your soul
And grace to your neck.

Proverbs 3:13–22

However, we speak wisdom among those who are mature, yet not the wisdom of this age, nor of the rulers of this age, who are coming to nothing.

But we speak the wisdom of God in a mystery, the hidden wisdom which God ordained before the ages for our glory,

which none of the rulers of this age knew; for had they known, they would not have crucified the Lord of glory.

But as it is written: "*Eye has not seen, nor ear heard,
Nor have entered into the heart of man
The things which God has prepared for those who love Him.*"

I Corinthians 2:6–9

But the wisdom that is from above is first pure, then peaceable, gentle, willing to yield, full of mercy and good fruits, without partiality and without hypocrisy.

James 3:17

If any of you lacks wisdom, let him ask of God, who gives to all liberally and without reproach, and it will be given to him.

But let him ask in faith, with no doubting, for he who doubts is like a wave of the sea driven and tossed by the wind.

James 1:5–6

His peace in troubled times

∞

The LORD builds up Jerusalem;
He gathers together the outcasts of Israel.
He heals the brokenhearted
And binds up their wounds.
Great is our Lord, and mighty in power;
His understanding is infinite.
The LORD lifts up the humble;
He casts the wicked down to the ground.
For He has strengthened the bars of your gates;
He has blessed your children within you.
He makes peace in your borders,
And fills you with the finest wheat.

Psalm 147:2–3, 5–6, 13–14

A horse is a vain hope for safety;
Neither shall it deliver any by its great strength.
Behold, the eye of the LORD is on those who fear
Him,
On those who hope in His mercy,
To deliver their soul from death,
And to keep them alive in famine.
Our soul waits for the LORD;

He is our help and our shield.
For our heart shall rejoice in Him,
Because we have trusted in His holy name.
Let Your mercy, O LORD, be upon us,
Just as we hope in You.

Psalm 33:17–22

Peace I leave with you, My peace I give to you; not as the world gives do I give to you. Let not your heart be troubled, neither let it be afraid.

John 14:27

Casting all your care upon Him, for He cares for you.

Be sober, be vigilant; because your adversary the devil walks about like a roaring lion, seeking whom he may devour.

Resist him, steadfast in the faith, knowing that the same sufferings are experienced by your brotherhood in the world.

But may the God of all grace, who called us to His eternal glory by Christ Jesus, after you have suffered a while, perfect, establish, strengthen, and settle you.

To Him be the glory and the dominion forever and ever. Amen.

I Peter 5:7–11

You are of God, little children, and have overcome them, because He who is in you is greater than he who is in the world.

I John 4:4

I will bless the LORD at all times;
His praise shall continually be in my mouth.
My soul shall make its boast in the LORD;
The humble shall hear of it and be glad.
Oh, magnify the LORD with me,
And let us exalt His name together.
I sought the LORD, and He heard me,
And delivered me from all my fears.
They looked to Him and were radiant,
And their faces were not ashamed.
This poor man cried out, and the LORD heard him,
And saved him out of all his troubles.
The angel of the LORD encamps all around those
who fear Him,
And delivers them.
Oh, taste and see that the LORD is good;
Blessed is the man who trusts in Him!

Psalm 34:1–8

Turn Yourself to me, and have mercy on me,
For I am desolate and afflicted.
The troubles of my heart have enlarged;

Bring me out of my distresses!
Look on my affliction and my pain,
And forgive all my sins.

Psalm 25:16–18

I will be glad and rejoice in Your mercy,
For You have considered my trouble;
You have known my soul in adversities.

Psalm 31:7

Victory over the sins in your life

∞

Therefore, if anyone is in Christ, he is a new creation; old things have passed away; behold, all things have become new.

Now all things are of God, who has reconciled us to Himself through Jesus Christ, and has given us the ministry of reconciliation,

that is, that God was in Christ reconciling the world to Himself, not imputing their trespasses to them, and has committed to us the word of reconciliation.

Now then, we are ambassadors for Christ, as though God were pleading through us: we implore you on Christ's behalf, be reconciled to God.

For He made Him who knew no sin to be sin for us, that we might become the righteousness of God in Him.

II Corinthians 5:17–21

O God, You know my foolishness;
And my sins are not hidden from You.

Psalm 69:5

"Wash yourselves, make yourselves clean;
Put away the evil of your doings from before My eyes.
Cease to do evil,

"Learn to do good;
Seek justice,
Rebuke the oppressor;
Defend the fatherless,
Plead for the widow.
Come now, and let us reason together,"
Says the LORD,
"Though your sins are like scarlet,
They shall be as white as snow;
Though they are red like crimson,
They shall be as wool.
If you are willing and obedient,
You shall eat the good of the land."

Isaiah 1:17–19

Therefore, since we have this ministry, as we have received mercy, we do not lose heart.

But we have renounced the hidden things of shame, not walking in craftiness nor handling the word of God deceitfully, but by manifestation of the truth commending ourselves to every man's conscience in the sight of God.

But even if our gospel is veiled, it is veiled to those who are perishing,

whose minds the god of this age has blinded, who do not believe, lest the light of the gospel of the glory of Christ, who is the image of God, should shine on them.

For we do not preach ourselves, but Christ Jesus the Lord, and ourselves your bondservants for Jesus' sake.

For it is the God who commanded light to shine out of darkness, who has shone in our hearts to give the light of the knowledge of the glory of God in the face of Jesus Christ.

II Corinthians 4:1–6

For as many as are of the works of the law are under the curse; for it is written, *"Cursed is everyone who does not continue in all things which are written in the book of the law, to do them."*

But that no one is justified by the law in the sight of God is evident, for *"the just shall live by faith."*

Galatians 3:10–11

This is the message which we have heard from Him and declare to you, that God is light and in Him is no darkness at all.

If we say that we have fellowship with Him, and walk in darkness, we lie and do not practice the truth.

But if we walk in the light as He is in the light, we have fellowship with one another, and the blood of Jesus Christ His Son cleanses us from all sin.

If we say that we have no sin, we deceive ourselves, and the truth is not in us.

If we confess our sins, He is faithful and just to forgive us our sins and to cleanse us from all unrighteousness.

If we say that we have not sinned, we make Him a liar, and His word is not in us.

I John 1:5–10

Stand fast therefore in the liberty by which Christ has made us free, and do not be entangled again with a yoke of bondage.

Galatians 5:1

"O Death, where is your sting?
O Hades, where is your victory?"
The sting of death is sin, and the strength of sin is the law.

But thanks be to God, who gives us the victory through our Lord Jesus Christ.

Therefore, my beloved brethren, be steadfast, immovable, always abounding in the work of the Lord, knowing that your labor is not in vain in the Lord.

I Corinthians 15:55–58

Finally, my brethren, be strong in the Lord and in the power of His might.

Put on the whole armor of God, that you may be able to stand against the wiles of the devil.

For we do not wrestle against flesh and blood, but against principalities, against powers, against the rulers of the darkness of this age, against spiritual hosts of wickedness in the heavenly places.

Therefore take up the whole armor of God, that you may be able to withstand in the evil day, and having done all, to stand.

Stand therefore, having girded your waist with truth, having put on the breastplate of righteousness,

and having shod your feet with the preparation of the gospel of peace;

above all, taking the shield of faith with which you will be able to quench all the fiery darts of the wicked one.

And take the helmet of salvation, and the sword of the Spirit, which is the word of God;

praying always with all prayer and supplication in the Spirit, being watchful to this end with all perseverance and supplication for all the saints.

Ephesians 6:10–18

Power to defeat
your deepest fears

∞

And God heard the voice of the lad. Then the angel of God called to Hagar out of heaven, and said to her, "What ails you, Hagar? Fear not, for God has heard the voice of the lad where he is.

"Arise, lift up the lad and hold him with your hand, for I will make him a great nation."

Then God opened her eyes, and she saw a well of water. And she went and filled the skin with water, and gave the lad a drink.

So God was with the lad; and he grew and dwelt in the wilderness, and became an archer.

Genesis 21:17–20

Oh, magnify the LORD with me,
And let us exalt His name together.
I sought the LORD, and He heard me,
And delivered me from all my fears.
They looked to Him and were radiant,
And their faces were not ashamed.
This poor man cried out, and the LORD heard him,
And saved him out of all his troubles.

The angel of the LORD encamps all around those
who fear Him,
And delivers them.
Oh, taste and see that the LORD is good;
Blessed is the man who trusts in Him!

Psalm 34:3–8

But Joshua the son of Nun and Caleb the son of
Jephunneh, who were among those who had spied out
the land, tore their clothes;

and they spoke to all the congregation of the children of Israel, saying: "The land we passed through to
spy out is an exceedingly good land.

"If the LORD delights in us, then He will bring us
into this land and give it to us, 'a land which flows with
milk and honey.'

"Only do not rebel against the LORD, nor fear the
people of the land, for they are our bread; their protec-
tion has departed from them, and the LORD is with us.
Do not fear them."

Numbers 14:6–9

Do not be afraid of sudden terror,
Nor of trouble from the wicked when it comes;
For the LORD will be your confidence,
And will keep your foot from being caught.

Proverbs 3:25–26

"'Look, the LORD your God has set the land before you; go up and possess it, as the LORD God of your fathers has spoken to you; do not fear or be discouraged.'

"And every one of you came near to me and said, 'Let us send men before us, and let them search out the land for us, and bring back word to us of the way by which we should go up, and of the cities into which we shall come.'

"The plan pleased me well; so I took twelve of your men, one man from each tribe.

"And they departed and went up into the mountains, and came to the Valley of Eshcol, and spied it out.

"They also took some of the fruit of the land in their hands and brought it down to us; and they brought back word to us, saying, 'It is a good land which the LORD our God is giving us.'

"Nevertheless you would not go up, but rebelled against the command of the LORD your God;

"and you complained in your tents, and said, 'Because the LORD hates us, He has brought us out of the land of Egypt to deliver us into the hand of the Amorites, to destroy us.

"'Where can we go up? Our brethren have discouraged our hearts, saying, "The people are greater and taller than we; the cities are great and fortified up to heaven; moreover we have seen the sons of the Anakim there."'"

"Then I said to you, 'Do not be terrified, or afraid of them.

"'The LORD your God, who goes before you, He will fight for you, according to all He did for you in Egypt before your eyes,

"'and in the wilderness where you saw how the LORD your God carried you, as a man carries his son, in all the way that you went until you came to this place.'"

Deuteronomy 1:21–31

After these things the word of the LORD came to Abram in a vision, saying, "Do not be afraid, Abram. I am your shield, your exceedingly great reward."

Genesis 15:1

Why should I fear in the days of evil,
When the iniquity at my heels surrounds me?
Those who trust in their wealth
And boast in the multitude of their riches . . .
But God will redeem my soul from the power of
the grave,
For He shall receive me. Selah
Do not be afraid when one becomes rich,
When the glory of his house is increased;
For when he dies he shall carry nothing away;
His glory shall not descend after him.

Psalm 49:5–6, 15–17

Yet in all these things we are more than conquerors through Him who loved us.

For I am persuaded that neither death nor life, nor angels nor principalities nor powers, nor things present nor things to come,

nor height nor depth, nor any other created thing, shall be able to separate us from the love of God which is in Christ Jesus our Lord.

Romans 8:37–39

The courage to be
a man of integrity

∞

Blessed is the man
Who walks not in the counsel of the ungodly,
Nor stands in the path of sinners,
Nor sits in the seat of the scornful;
But his delight is in the law of the LORD,
And in His law he meditates day and night.
He shall be like a tree
Planted by the rivers of water,
That brings forth its fruit in its season,
Whose leaf also shall not wither;
And whatever he does shall prosper.
The ungodly are not so,
But are like the chaff which the wind drives away.
Therefore the ungodly shall not stand in the judgment,
Nor sinners in the congregation of the righteous.
For the LORD knows the way of the righteous,
But the way of the ungodly shall perish.

Psalm 1:1–6

A good man deals graciously and lends;
He will guide his affairs with discretion.

Surely he will never be shaken;
The righteous will be in everlasting remembrance.
He will not be afraid of evil tidings;
His heart is steadfast, trusting in the LORD.

Psalm 112:5–7

Blessed are the undefiled in the way,
Who walk in the law of the LORD!
Blessed are those who keep His testimonies,
Who seek Him with the whole heart!
They also do no iniquity;
They walk in His ways.
You have commanded us
To keep Your precepts diligently.
Oh, that my ways were directed
To keep Your statutes!
Then I would not be ashamed,
When I look into all Your commandments.
I will praise You with uprightness of heart,
When I learn Your righteous judgments.
I will keep Your statutes;
Oh, do not forsake me utterly!

Psalm 119:1–8

Then Phinehas stood up and intervened,
And the plague was stopped.

And that was accounted to him for righteousness
To all generations forevermore.

Psalm 106:30–31

Dishonest scales are an abomination to the LORD,
But a just weight is His delight.
When pride comes, then comes shame;
But with the humble is wisdom.
The integrity of the upright will guide them,
But the perversity of the unfaithful will destroy them.

Proverbs 11:1–3

Diverse weights are an abomination to the LORD,
And dishonest scales are not good.

Proverbs 20:23

He who speaks truth declares righteousness,
But a false witness, deceit.
There is one who speaks like the piercings of a sword,
But the tongue of the wise promotes health.
The truthful lip shall be established forever,
But a lying tongue is but for a moment.

Proverbs 12:17–19

The LORD shall judge the peoples;
Judge me, O LORD, according to my righteousness,
And according to my integrity within me.

Psalm 7:8

I will behave wisely in a perfect way.
Oh, when will You come to me?
I will walk within my house with a perfect heart.
I will set nothing wicked before my eyes;
I hate the work of those who fall away;
It shall not cling to me.
A perverse heart shall depart from me;
I will not know wickedness.
Whoever secretly slanders his neighbor,
Him I will destroy;
The one who has a haughty look and a proud
heart,
Him I will not endure.
My eyes shall be on the faithful of the land,
That they may dwell with me;
He who walks in a perfect way,
He shall serve me.
He who works deceit shall not dwell within my
house;
He who tells lies shall not continue in my presence.
Early I will destroy all the wicked of the land,
That I may cut off all the evildoers from the city
of the LORD.

Psalm 101:2–8

GOD ASKS
YOU TO

Instruct your children
in His Word

∞

Hear, my children, the instruction of a father,
And give attention to know understanding;
For I give you good doctrine:
Do not forsake my law.
When I was my father's son,
Tender and the only one in the sight of my mother,
He also taught me, and said to me:
"Let your heart retain my words;
Keep my commands, and live."

Proverbs 4:1–4

Give ear, O my people, to my law;
Incline your ears to the words of my mouth.
I will open my mouth in a parable;
I will utter dark sayings of old,
Which we have heard and known,
And our fathers have told us.
We will not hide them from their children,
Telling to the generation to come the praises of
the LORD,

And His strength and His wonderful works that He
has done.
For He established a testimony in Jacob,
And appointed a law in Israel,
Which He commanded our fathers,
That they should make them known to their children;
That the generation to come might know them,
The children who would be born,
That they may arise and declare them to their children,
That they may set their hope in God,
And not forget the works of God,
But keep His commandments;
And may not be like their fathers,
A stubborn and rebellious generation,
A generation that did not set its heart aright,
And whose spirit was not faithful to God.

Psalm 78:1–8

A wise man will hear and increase learning,
And a man of understanding will attain wise counsel,
To understand a proverb and an enigma,
The words of the wise and their riddles.
The fear of the LORD is the beginning of knowledge,
But fools despise wisdom and instruction.
My son, hear the instruction of your father,
And do not forsake the law of your mother;

For they will be a graceful ornament on your head,
And chains about your neck.

Proverbs 1:5–9

I do not write these things to shame you, but as my beloved children I warn you.

For though you might have ten thousand instructors in Christ, yet you do not have many fathers; for in Christ Jesus I have begotten you through the gospel.

Therefore I urge you, imitate me.

For this reason I have sent Timothy to you, who is my beloved and faithful son in the Lord, who will remind you of my ways in Christ, as I teach everywhere in every church.

Now some are puffed up, as though I were not coming to you.

But I will come to you shortly, if the Lord wills, and I will know, not the word of those who are puffed up, but the power.

For the kingdom of God is not in word but in power.

What do you want? Shall I come to you with a rod, or in love and a spirit of gentleness?

I Corinthians 4:14–21

Now therefore, listen to me, my children,
For blessed are those who keep my ways.
Hear instruction and be wise,
And do not disdain it.

Blessed is the man who listens to me,
Watching daily at my gates,
Waiting at the posts of my doors.
For whoever finds me finds life,
And obtains favor from the LORD.

Proverbs 8:32–35

All Scripture is given by inspiration of God, and is profitable for doctrine, for reproof, for correction, for instruction in righteousness.

II Timothy 3:16

For the word of God is living and powerful, and sharper than any two-edged sword, piercing even to the division of soul and spirit, and of joints and marrow, and is a discerner of the thoughts and intents of the heart.

Hebrews 4:12

But be doers of the word, and not hearers only, deceiving yourselves.

James 1:22

My son, give attention to my words;
Incline your ear to my sayings.
Do not let them depart from your eyes;
Keep them in the midst of your heart;
For they are life to those who find them,
And health to all their flesh.

Proverbs 4:20–22

Therefore, laying aside all malice, all deceit, hypocrisy, envy, and all evil speaking, as newborn babes, desire the pure milk of the word, that you may grow thereby.

I Peter 2:1–2

Because
"All flesh is as grass,
And all the glory of man as the flower of the grass.
The grass withers,
And its flower falls away,
But the word of the LORD endures forever."
Now this is the word which by the gospel was preached to you.

I Peter 1:24–25

I will go in the strength of the Lord GOD;
I will make mention of Your righteousness, of
Yours only.
O God, You have taught me from my youth;
And to this day I declare Your wondrous works.
Now also when I am old and grayheaded,
O God, do not forsake me,
Until I declare Your strength to this generation,
Your power to everyone who is to come.

Psalm 71:16–18

Teach your children to pray

∞

But will God indeed dwell on the earth? Behold, heaven and the heaven of heavens cannot contain You. How much less this temple which I have built!

Yet regard the prayer of Your servant and his supplication, O LORD my God, and listen to the cry and the prayer which Your servant is praying before You today:

that Your eyes may be open toward this temple night and day, toward the place of which You said, "My name shall be there," that You may hear the prayer which Your servant makes toward this place.

And may You hear the supplication of Your servant and of Your people Israel, when they pray toward this place. Hear in heaven Your dwelling place; and when You hear, forgive.

I Kings 8:27–30

Let us therefore come boldly to the throne of grace, that we may obtain mercy and find grace to help in time of need.

Hebrews 4:16

For You, O LORD of hosts, God of Israel, have revealed this to Your servant, saying, "I will build you a house." Therefore Your servant has found it in his heart to pray this prayer to You.

And now, O Lord GOD, You are God, and Your words are true, and You have promised this goodness to Your servant.

II Samuel 7:27–28

Therefore I say to you, whatever things you ask when you pray, believe that you receive them, and you will have them.

Mark 11:24

Call to Me, and I will answer you, and show you great and mighty things, which you do not know.

Jeremiah 33:3

For we were saved in this hope, but hope that is seen is not hope; for why does one still hope for what he sees?

But if we hope for what we do not see, we eagerly wait for it with perseverance.

Likewise the Spirit also helps in our weaknesses. For we do not know what we should pray for as we ought, but the Spirit Himself makes intercession for us with groanings which cannot be uttered.

Now He who searches the hearts knows what the mind of the Spirit is, because He makes intercession for the saints according to the will of God.

And we know that all things work together for good to those who love God, to those who are the called according to His purpose.

Romans 8:24–28

And whatever we ask we receive from Him, because we keep His commandments and do those things that are pleasing in His sight.

I John 3:22

And when you pray, you shall not be like the hypocrites. For they love to pray standing in the synagogues and on the corners of the streets, that they may be seen by men. Assuredly, I say to you, they have their reward.

But you, when you pray, go into your room, and when you have shut your door, pray to your Father who is in the secret place; and your Father who sees in secret will reward you openly.

And when you pray, do not use vain repetitions as the heathen do. For they think that they will be heard for their many words.

Therefore do not be like them. For your Father knows the things you have need of before you ask Him.

In this manner, therefore, pray:

Our Father in heaven,

Hallowed be Your name.

Your kingdom come.
Your will be done
On earth as it is in heaven.
Give us this day our daily bread.
And forgive us our debts,
As we forgive our debtors.
And do not lead us into temptation,
But deliver us from the evil one.
For Yours is the kingdom and the power and the
glory forever. Amen.

Matthew 6:5–13

It shall come to pass
That before they call, I will answer;
And while they are still speaking,
I will hear.

Isaiah 65:24

These things I have written to you who believe in the name of the Son of God, that you may know that you have eternal life, and that you may continue to believe in the name of the Son of God.

Now this is the confidence that we have in Him, that if we ask anything according to His will, He hears us.

And if we know that He hears us, whatever we ask, we know that we have the petitions that we have asked of Him.

I John 5:13–15

Reach out to families
who are homeless

∞

You shall rejoice before the LORD your God, you and your son and your daughter, your male servant and your female servant, the Levite who is within your gates, the stranger and the fatherless and the widow who are among you, at the place where the LORD your God chooses to make His name abide.

Deuteronomy 16:11

Whoever shuts his ears to the cry of the poor
Will also cry himself and not be heard.

Proverbs 21:13

Yet they seek Me daily,
And delight to know My ways,
As a nation that did righteousness,
And did not forsake the ordinance of their God.
They ask of Me the ordinances of justice;
They take delight in approaching God.

Isaiah 58:2

Is it not to share your bread with the hungry,
And that you bring to your house the poor who are cast out;

When you see the naked, that you cover him,
And not hide yourself from your own flesh?
Then your light shall break forth like the morning,
Your healing shall spring forth speedily,
And your righteousness shall go before you;
The glory of the LORD shall be your rear guard.
Then you shall call, and the LORD will answer;
You shall cry, and He will say, "Here I am."
If you take away the yoke from your midst,
The pointing of the finger, and speaking wickedness,
If you extend your soul to the hungry
And satisfy the afflicted soul,
Then your light shall dawn in the darkness,
And your darkness shall be as the noonday.
The LORD will guide you continually,
And satisfy your soul in drought,
And strengthen your bones;
You shall be like a watered garden,
And like a spring of water, whose waters do not fail.

Isaiah 58:7–11

Then the King will say to those on His right hand,
"Come, you blessed of My Father, inherit the kingdom
prepared for you from the foundation of the world:

"For I was hungry and you gave Me food; I was
thirsty and you gave Me drink; I was a stranger and you
took Me in;

"I was naked and you clothed Me; I was sick and you visited Me; I was in prison and you came to Me."

Then the righteous will answer Him, saying, "Lord, when did we see You hungry and feed You, or thirsty and give You drink?

"When did we see You a stranger and take You in, or naked and clothe You?

"Or when did we see You sick, or in prison, and come to You?"

And the King will answer and say to them, "Assuredly, I say to you, inasmuch as you did it to one of the least of these My brethren, you did it to Me."

Matthew 25:34–40

Happy is he who has the God of Jacob for his help,
Whose hope is in the LORD his God,
Who made heaven and earth,
The sea, and all that is in them;
Who keeps truth forever,
Who executes justice for the oppressed,
Who gives food to the hungry.
The LORD gives freedom to the prisoners.
The LORD opens the eyes of the blind;
The LORD raises those who are bowed down;
The LORD loves the righteous.
The LORD watches over the strangers;
He relieves the fatherless and widow;

But the way of the wicked He turns upside down.
The LORD shall reign forever—
Your God, O Zion, to all generations.
Praise the LORD!

Psalm 146:5–10

Let brotherly love continue.

Do not forget to entertain strangers, for by so doing some have unwittingly entertained angels.

Hebrews 13:1–2

And above all things have fervent love for one another, for *"love will cover a multitude of sins."*

Be hospitable to one another without grumbling.

As each one has received a gift, minister it to one another, as good stewards of the manifold grace of God.

I Peter 4:8–10

But whoever has this world's goods, and sees his brother in need, and shuts up his heart from him, how does the love of God abide in him?

My little children, let us not love in word or in tongue, but in deed and in truth.

And by this we know that we are of the truth, and shall assure our hearts before Him.

I John 3:17–19

When you reap the harvest of your land, you shall not wholly reap the corners of your field, nor shall you gather the gleanings of your harvest.

And you shall not glean your vineyard, nor shall you gather every grape of your vineyard; you shall leave them for the poor and the stranger: I am the LORD your God.

Leviticus 19:9–10

Love your neighbors

∞

You shall love your neighbor as yourself.

Matthew 19:19b

Do not say to your neighbor,
"Go, and come back,
And tomorrow I will give it,"
When you have it with you.
Do not devise evil against your neighbor,
For he dwells by you for safety's sake.

Proverbs 3:28–29

He who despises his neighbor sins;
But he who has mercy on the poor, happy is he.

Proverbs 14:21

He who is devoid of wisdom despises his neighbor,
But a man of understanding holds his peace.

Proverbs 11:12

You shall not cheat your neighbor, nor rob him.

Leviticus 19:13a

Do not go hastily to court;
For what will you do in the end,
When your neighbor has put you to shame?
Debate your case with your neighbor,
And do not disclose the secret to another.

Proverbs 25:8–9

You shall not bear false witness against your neighbor.

You shall not covet your neighbor's house; you shall not covet your neighbor's wife, nor his male servant, nor his female servant, nor his ox, nor his donkey, nor anything that is your neighbor's.

Exodus 20:16–17

Whoever secretly slanders his neighbor,
Him I will destroy;
The one who has a haughty look and a proud heart,
Him I will not endure.
My eyes shall be on the faithful of the land,
That they may dwell with me;
He who walks in a perfect way, he shall serve me.
He who works deceit shall not dwell within my house;
He who tells lies shall not continue in my presence.

Psalm 101:5–7

And do not be conformed to this world, but be transformed by the renewing of your mind, that you may prove what is that good and acceptable and perfect will of God.

For I say, through the grace given to me, to everyone who is among you, not to think of himself more highly than he ought to think, but to think soberly, as God has dealt to each one a measure of faith.

Romans 12:2–3

But he, wanting to justify himself, said to Jesus, "And who is my neighbor?"

Then Jesus answered and said: "A certain man went down from Jerusalem to Jericho, and fell among thieves, who stripped him of his clothing, wounded him, and departed, leaving him half dead.

"Now by chance a certain priest came down that road. And when he saw him, he passed by on the other side.

"Likewise a Levite, when he arrived at the place, came and looked, and passed by on the other side.

"But a certain Samaritan, as he journeyed, came where he was. And when he saw him, he had compassion.

"So he went to him and bandaged his wounds, pouring on oil and wine; and he set him on his own animal, brought him to an inn, and took care of him.

"On the next day, when he departed, he took out two denarii, gave them to the innkeeper, and said to him, 'Take care of him; and whatever more you spend, when I come again, I will repay you.'

"So which of these three do you think was neighbor to him who fell among the thieves?"

And he said, "He who showed mercy on him." Then Jesus said to him, "Go and do likewise."

Luke 10:29–37

Teach your children gratitude
∞

If indeed you have tasted that the Lord is gracious.
I Peter 2:3

Make a joyful shout to the LORD, all you lands!
Serve the LORD with gladness;
Come before His presence with singing.
Psalm 100:1–2

And that their children, who have not known it, may hear and learn to fear the LORD your God as long as you live in the land which you cross the Jordan to possess.
Deuteronomy 31:13

Now therefore, write down this song for yourselves, and teach it to the children of Israel; put it in their mouths, that this song may be a witness for Me against the children of Israel.

When I have brought them to the land flowing with milk and honey, of which I swore to their fathers, and they have eaten and filled themselves and grown fat, then they will turn to other gods and serve them; and they will provoke Me and break My covenant.

Then it shall be, when many evils and troubles have come upon them, that this song will testify against them as a witness; for it will not be forgotten in the mouths of their descendants, for I know the inclination of their behavior today, even before I have brought them to the land of which I swore to give them.

Deuteronomy 31:19–21

Let your conduct be without covetousness; be content with such things as you have. For He Himself has said, *"I will never leave you nor forsake you."*

Hebrews 13:5

And my spirit has rejoiced in God my Savior.

Luke 1:47

Finally, brethren, whatever things are true, whatever things are noble, whatever things are just, whatever things are pure, whatever things are lovely, whatever things are of good report, if there is any virtue and if there is anything praiseworthy—meditate on these things.

The things which you learned and received and heard and saw in me, these do, and the God of peace will be with you.

But I rejoiced in the Lord greatly that now at last your care for me has flourished again; though you surely did care, but you lacked opportunity.

Not that I speak in regard to need, for I have learned in whatever state I am, to be content.

Philippians 4:8–11

Sing praise to the LORD, you saints of His,
And give thanks at the remembrance of His holy name.
For His anger is but for a moment,
His favor is for life;
Weeping may endure for a night,
But joy comes in the morning.
Now in my prosperity I said,
"I shall never be moved."

Psalm 30:4–6

Now it happened as He went to Jerusalem that He passed through the midst of Samaria and Galilee.

Then as He entered a certain village, there met Him ten men who were lepers, who stood afar off.

And they lifted up their voices and said, "Jesus, Master, have mercy on us!"

So when He saw them, He said to them, "Go, show yourselves to the priests." And so it was that as they went, they were cleansed.

And one of them, when he saw that he was healed, returned, and with a loud voice glorified God, and fell down on his face at His feet, giving Him thanks. And he was a Samaritan.

So Jesus answered and said, "Were there not ten cleansed? But where are the nine?

"Were there not any found who returned to give glory to God except this foreigner?"

And He said to him, "Arise, go your way. Your faith has made you well."

Luke 17:11–19

But I determined this within myself, that I would not come again to you in sorrow.

For if I make you sorrowful, then who is he who makes me glad but the one who is made sorrowful by me?

And I wrote this very thing to you, lest, when I came, I should have sorrow over those from whom I ought to have joy, having confidence in you all that my joy is the joy of you all.

II Corinthians 2:1–3

Show kindness to your family

∞

Or what man is there among you who, if his son asks for bread, will give him a stone?

Or if he asks for a fish, will he give him a serpent?

If you then, being evil, know how to give good gifts to your children, how much more will your Father who is in heaven give good things to those who ask Him!

Matthew 7:9–11

Then his father Isaac said to him, "Come near now and kiss me, my son."

Genesis 27:26

I traverse the way of righteousness,
In the midst of the paths of justice,
That I may cause those who love me to inherit wealth,
That I may fill their treasuries.
"The LORD possessed me at the beginning of His way,
Before His works of old."

Proverbs 8:20–22

"Now therefore, I beg you, swear to me by the LORD, since I have shown you kindness, that you also will show kindness to my father's house, and give me a true token,

"and spare my father, my mother, my brothers, my sisters, and all that they have, and deliver our lives from death."

So the men answered her, "Our lives for yours, if none of you tell this business of ours. And it shall be, when the LORD has given us the land, that we will deal kindly and truly with you."

Joshua 2:12–14

Whoever has no rule over his own spirit
Is like a city broken down, without walls.

Proverbs 25:28

Yet it shall not be so among you; but whoever desires to become great among you shall be your servant.

And whoever of you desires to be first shall be slave of all.

For even the Son of Man did not come to be served, but to serve, and to give His life a ransom for many.

Mark 10:43–45

Do not be overcome by evil, but overcome evil with good.

Romans 12:21

Let all bitterness, wrath, anger, clamor, and evil speaking be put away from you, with all malice.

And be kind to one another, tenderhearted, forgiving one another, even as God in Christ forgave you.

Ephesians 4:31–32

And Naomi said to her two daughters-in-law, "Go, return each to her mother's house. The LORD deal kindly with you, as you have dealt with the dead and with me."

Ruth 1:8

Hatred stirs up strife,
But love covers all sins.

Proverbs 10:12

We then who are strong ought to bear with the scruples of the weak, and not to please ourselves.

Romans 15:1

Joseph said to them, "Do not be afraid, for am I in the place of God?

"But as for you, you meant evil against me; but God meant it for good, in order to bring it about as it is this day, to save many people alive.

"Now therefore, do not be afraid; I will provide for you and your little ones."

And he comforted them and spoke kindly to them.

Genesis 50:19–21

You are witnesses, and God also, how devoutly and justly and blamelessly we behaved ourselves among you who believe;

as you know how we exhorted, and comforted, and charged every one of you, as a father does his own children,

that you would walk worthy of God who calls you into His own kingdom and glory.

I Thessalonians 2:10–12

Trust Him even when you don't understand

∞

Behold, He who keeps Israel
Shall neither slumber nor sleep.
The LORD is your keeper;
The LORD is your shade at your right hand.
The sun shall not strike you by day,
Nor the moon by night.
The LORD shall preserve you from all evil;
He shall preserve your soul.
The LORD shall preserve your going out and your coming in
From this time forth, and even forevermore.

Psalm 121:4–8

Some trust in chariots, and some in horses;
But we will remember the name of the LORD our God.
They have bowed down and fallen;
But we have risen and stand upright.
Save, LORD!
May the King answer us when we call.

Psalm 20:7–9

"Even now men cannot look at the light when it
is bright in the skies,
When the wind has passed and cleared them.
"He comes from the north as golden splendor;
With God is awesome majesty.
"As for the Almighty, we cannot find Him;
He is excellent in power,
In judgment and abundant justice;
He does not oppress.
"Therefore men fear Him;
He shows no partiality to any who are wise of heart."

Job 37:21–24

Oh, the depth of the riches both of the wisdom and
knowledge of God! How unsearchable are His judg-
ments and His ways past finding out!
"For who has known the mind of the LORD?
Or who has become His counselor?"
"Or who has first given to Him
And it shall be repaid to him?"
For of Him and through Him and to Him are all
things, to whom be glory forever. Amen.

Romans 11:33–36

Then Job answered and said:
"Even today my complaint is bitter;
My hand is listless because of my groaning.
Oh, that I knew where I might find Him,

That I might come to His seat!
I would present my case before Him,
And fill my mouth with arguments.
I would know the words which He would answer me,
And understand what He would say to me.
Would He contend with me in His great power?
No! But He would take note of me.
There the upright could reason with Him,
And I would be delivered forever from my Judge.
Look, I go forward, but He is not there,
And backward, but I cannot perceive Him;
When He works on the left hand, I cannot
behold Him;
When He turns to the right hand, I cannot see Him.
But He knows the way that I take;
When He has tested me, I shall come forth as gold.
My foot has held fast to His steps;
I have kept His way and not turned aside.
I have not departed from the commandment of
His lips;
I have treasured the words of His mouth more
than my necessary food."

Job 23:1–12

In the day of my trouble I will call upon You,
For You will answer me.
Among the gods there is none like You, O Lord;

Nor are there any works like Your works.
All nations whom You have made
Shall come and worship before You, O Lord,
And shall glorify Your name.
For You are great, and do wondrous things;
You alone are God.

Psalm 86:7–10

Then they cried out to the LORD in their trouble,
And He saved them out of their distresses.
He sent His word and healed them,
And delivered them from their destructions.

Psalm 107:19–20

Every word of God is pure;
He is a shield to those who put their trust in Him.

Proverbs 30:5

Therefore, brethren, in all our affliction and distress we were comforted concerning you by your faith.
For now we live, if you stand fast in the Lord.

I Thessalonians 3:7–8

Speak encouraging words to all
∞

Therefore, as we have opportunity, let us do good to all, especially to those who are of the household of faith.
Galatians 6:10

Let no corrupt word proceed out of your mouth, but what is good for necessary edification, that it may impart grace to the hearers.

And do not grieve the Holy Spirit of God, by whom you were sealed for the day of redemption.

Let all bitterness, wrath, anger, clamor, and evil speaking be put away from you, with all malice.

And be kind to one another, tenderhearted, forgiving one another, even as God in Christ forgave you.
Ephesians 4:29–32

Bear one another's burdens, and so fulfill the law of Christ.

Galatians 6:2

If anyone among you thinks he is religious, and does not bridle his tongue but deceives his own heart, this one's religion is useless.

James 1:26

For we all stumble in many things. If anyone does not stumble in word, he is a perfect man, able also to bridle the whole body.

Indeed, we put bits in horses' mouths that they may obey us, and we turn their whole body.

Look also at ships: although they are so large and are driven by fierce winds, they are turned by a very small rudder wherever the pilot desires.

Even so the tongue is a little member and boasts great things. See how great a forest a little fire kindles!

And the tongue is a fire, a world of iniquity. The tongue is so set among our members that it defiles the whole body, and sets on fire the course of nature; and it is set on fire by hell.

For every kind of beast and bird, of reptile and creature of the sea, is tamed and has been tamed by mankind.

But no man can tame the tongue. It is an unruly evil, full of deadly poison.

With it we bless our God and Father, and with it we curse men, who have been made in the similitude of God.

Out of the same mouth proceed blessing and cursing. My brethren, these things ought not to be so.

James 3:2–10

Not returning evil for evil or reviling for reviling, but on the contrary blessing, knowing that you were called to this, that you may inherit a blessing.

For

"He who would love life
And see good days,
Let him refrain his tongue from evil,
And his lips from speaking deceit."

I Peter 3:9–10

There is one who speaks like the piercings of a sword,
But the tongue of the wise promotes health.

Proverbs 12:18

A man has joy by the answer of his mouth,
And a word spoken in due season, how good it is!

Proverbs 15:23

The wilderness and the wasteland shall be glad for
them,
And the desert shall rejoice and blossom as the rose;
It shall blossom abundantly and rejoice,
Even with joy and singing.
The glory of Lebanon shall be given to it,
The excellence of Carmel and Sharon.
They shall see the glory of the LORD,
The excellency of our God.
Strengthen the weak hands,
And make firm the feeble knees.
Say to those who are fearful-hearted,
"Be strong, do not fear!

Behold, your God will come with vengeance,
With the recompense of God;
He will come and save you."

Isaiah 35:1–4

For out of the abundance of the heart the mouth speaks.

But I say to you that for every idle word men may speak, they will give account of it in the day of judgment.

For by your words you will be justified, and by your words you will be condemned.

Matthew 12:34b, 36–37

We took sweet counsel together,
And walked to the house of God in the throng.

Psalm 55:14

For none of us lives to himself, and no one dies to himself.

For if we live, we live to the Lord; and if we die, we die to the Lord. Therefore, whether we live or die, we are the Lord's.

For to this end Christ died and rose and lived again, that He might be Lord of both the dead and the living.

But why do you judge your brother? Or why do you show contempt for your brother? For we shall all stand before the judgment seat of Christ.

For it is written:
"*As I live, says the LORD,*
Every knee shall bow to Me,
And every tongue shall confess to God."
So then each of us shall give account of himself to God.

Therefore let us not judge one another anymore, but rather resolve this, not to put a stumbling block or a cause to fall in our brother's way.

I know and am convinced by the Lord Jesus that there is nothing unclean of itself; but to him who considers anything to be unclean, to him it is unclean.

Yet if your brother is grieved because of your food, you are no longer walking in love. Do not destroy with your food the one for whom Christ died.

Therefore do not let your good be spoken of as evil; for the kingdom of God is not eating and drinking, but righteousness and peace and joy in the Holy Spirit.

For he who serves Christ in these things is acceptable to God and approved by men.

Therefore let us pursue the things which make for peace and the things by which one may edify another.

Romans 14:7–19

GOD GIVES YOU STRENGTH WHEN

You comfort your children in their sorrows

∞

But the mercy of the LORD is from everlasting to
everlasting
On those who fear Him,
And His righteousness to children's children.

Psalm 103:17

He will feed His flock like a shepherd;
He will gather the lambs with His arm,
And carry them in His bosom,
And gently lead those who are with young.

Isaiah 40:11

"Comfort, yes, comfort My people!"
Says your God.
The grass withers, the flower fades,
But the word of our God stands forever.

Isaiah 40:1, 8

Fear not, for I am with you;
Be not dismayed, for I am your God.
I will strengthen you,
Yes, I will help you,

I will uphold you with My righteous right hand.
Behold, I will make you into a new threshing sledge
with sharp teeth;
You shall thresh the mountains and beat them small,
And make the hills like chaff.
You shall winnow them,
The wind shall carry them away,
And the whirlwind shall scatter them;
You shall rejoice in the LORD,
And glory in the Holy One of Israel.

Isaiah 41:10, 15–16

Surely He has borne our griefs
And carried our sorrows;
Yet we esteemed Him stricken,
Smitten by God, and afflicted.
But He was wounded for our transgressions,
He was bruised for our iniquities;
The chastisement for our peace was upon Him,
And by His stripes we are healed.

Isaiah 53:4–5

When the waves of death surrounded me,
The floods of ungodliness made me afraid.
The sorrows of Sheol surrounded me;
The snares of death confronted me.
In my distress I called upon the LORD,

And cried out to my God;
He heard my voice from His temple,
And my cry entered His ears.

II Samuel 22:5–7

The Lord GOD, who gathers the outcasts of Israel, says,
"Yet I will gather to him
Others besides those who are gathered to him."

Isaiah 56:8

Sing, O heavens!
Be joyful, O earth!
And break out in singing, O mountains!
For the LORD has comforted His people,
And will have mercy on His afflicted.
But Zion said, "The LORD has forsaken me,
And my Lord has forgotten me.
Can a woman forget her nursing child,
And not have compassion on the son of her womb?
Surely they may forget,
Yet I will not forget you.
See, I have inscribed you on the palms of My hands;
Your walls are continually before Me."

Isaiah 49:13–16

For I have satiated the weary soul, and I have replenished every sorrowful soul.

Jeremiah 31:25

Are not two sparrows sold for a copper coin? And not one of them falls to the ground apart from your Father's will.

But the very hairs of your head are all numbered.

Do not fear therefore; you are of more value than many sparrows.

Matthew 10:29–31

Blessed be the God and Father of our Lord Jesus Christ, the Father of mercies and God of all comfort,

who comforts us in all our tribulation, that we may be able to comfort those who are in any trouble, with the comfort with which we ourselves are comforted by God.

For as the sufferings of Christ abound in us, so our consolation also abounds through Christ.

II Corinthians 1:3–5

You feel defeated and powerless

∞

God is our refuge and strength, a very present
help in trouble.
Therefore we will not fear,
Even though the earth be removed,
And though the mountains be carried into the
midst of the sea;
Though its waters roar and be troubled,
Though the mountains shake with its swelling. Selah

Psalm 46:1–3

"For affliction does not come from the dust,
Nor does trouble spring from the ground;
Yet man is born to trouble,
As the sparks fly upward.
But as for me, I would seek God,
And to God I would commit my cause—
Who does great things, and unsearchable,
Marvelous things without number."

Job 5:6–9

Give ear to my words, O LORD,
Consider my meditation.

Give heed to the voice of my cry,
My King and my God,
For to You I will pray.
My voice You shall hear in the morning, O LORD;
In the morning I will direct it to You,
And I will look up.
For You are not a God who takes pleasure in
wickedness,
Nor shall evil dwell with You.
The boastful shall not stand in Your sight;
You hate all workers of iniquity.
You shall destroy those who speak falsehood;
The LORD abhors the bloodthirsty and deceitful man.
But as for me, I will come into Your house in the
multitude of Your mercy;
In fear of You I will worship toward Your holy temple.
Lead me, O LORD, in Your righteousness because
of my enemies;
Make Your way straight before my face.
But let all those rejoice who put their trust in You;
Let them ever shout for joy, because You defend
them;
Let those also who love Your name
Be joyful in You.
For You, O LORD, will bless the righteous;
With favor You will surround him as with a shield.

Psalm 5:1–8, 11–12

Concerning this thing I pleaded with the Lord three times that it might depart from me.

And He said to me, "My grace is sufficient for you, for My strength is made perfect in weakness." Therefore most gladly I will rather boast in my infirmities, that the power of Christ may rest upon me.

Therefore I take pleasure in infirmities, in reproaches, in needs, in persecutions, in distresses, for Christ's sake. For when I am weak, then I am strong.

II Corinthians 12:8–10

And those who know Your name will put their
trust in You;
For You, LORD, have not forsaken those who seek
You.

Psalm 9:10

You are my hiding place and my shield;
I hope in Your word.

Psalm 119:114

Give us help from trouble,
For the help of man is useless.
Through God we will do valiantly,
For it is He who shall tread down our enemies.

Psalm 108:12–13

He who dwells in the secret place of the Most High
Shall abide under the shadow of the Almighty.

I will say of the LORD,
"He is my refuge and my fortress;
My God, in Him I will trust."
Surely He shall deliver you from the snare of the
fowler
And from the perilous pestilence.
He shall cover you with His feathers,
And under His wings you shall take refuge;
His truth shall be your shield and buckler.
You shall not be afraid of the terror by night,
Nor of the arrow that flies by day,
Nor of the pestilence that walks in darkness,
Nor of the destruction that lays waste at noonday.
A thousand may fall at your side,
And ten thousand at your right hand;
But it shall not come near you.
Only with your eyes shall you look,
And see the reward of the wicked.
Because you have made the LORD,
Who is my refuge,
Even the Most High, your dwelling place,
No evil shall befall you,
Nor shall any plague come near your dwelling.

Psalm 91:1–10

Bow down Your ear, O LORD, hear me;
For I am poor and needy.

Preserve my life, for I am holy;
You are my God;
Save Your servant who trusts in You!
Be merciful to me, O Lord,
For I cry to You all day long.
Rejoice the soul of Your servant,
For to You, O Lord, I lift up my soul.
For You, Lord, are good, and ready to forgive,
And abundant in mercy to all those who call upon
You.
Give ear, O LORD, to my prayer;
And attend to the voice of my supplications.

Psalm 86:1–6

You are my God, and I will praise You;
You are my God, I will exalt You.

Psalm 118:28

Trouble and anguish have overtaken me,
Yet Your commandments are my delights.
The righteousness of Your testimonies is everlasting;
Give me understanding, and I shall live.

Psalm 119:143–144

I cried out to You, O LORD:
I said, "You are my refuge,
My portion in the land of the living.

Attend to my cry,
For I am brought very low;
Deliver me from my persecutors,
For they are stronger than I.
Bring my soul out of prison,
That I may praise Your name;
The righteous shall surround me,
For You shall deal bountifully with me."

Psalm 142:5–7

And I, brethren, when I came to you, did not come with excellence of speech or of wisdom declaring to you the testimony of God.

For I determined not to know anything among you except Jesus Christ and Him crucified.

I was with you in weakness, in fear, and in much trembling.

And my speech and my preaching were not with persuasive words of human wisdom, but in demonstration of the Spirit and of power,

that your faith should not be in the wisdom of men but in the power of God.

I Corinthians 2:1–5

Let this mind be in you which was also in Christ Jesus,

who, being in the form of God, did not consider it robbery to be equal with God,

But made Himself of no reputation, taking the form of a bondservant, and coming in the likeness of men.

And being found in appearance as a man, He humbled Himself and became obedient to the point of death, even the death of the cross.

Therefore God also has highly exalted Him and given Him the name which is above every name.

Philippians 2:5–9

Your children disobey you

∞

Children, obey your parents in the Lord, for this is right.

And you, fathers, do not provoke your children to wrath, but bring them up in the training and admonition of the Lord.

Ephesians 6:1, 4

But You, O Lord, are a God full of compassion, and gracious,
Longsuffering and abundant in mercy and truth.
Oh, turn to me, and have mercy on me!
Give Your strength to Your servant,
And save the son of Your maidservant.

Psalm 86:15–16

If his sons forsake My law
And do not walk in My judgments,
If they break My statutes
And do not keep My commandments,
Then I will punish their transgression with the rod,
And their iniquity with stripes.
Nevertheless My lovingkindness I will not utterly take from him,

Nor allow My faithfulness to fail.
My covenant I will not break,
Nor alter the word that has gone out of My lips.

Psalm 89:30–34

Though He was a Son, yet He learned obedience by
the things which He suffered.

Hebrews 5:8

As a father pities his children,
So the LORD pities those who fear Him.
For He knows our frame;
He remembers that we are dust.
As for man, his days are like grass;
As a flower of the field, so he flourishes.
For the wind passes over it, and it is gone,
And its place remembers it no more.
But the mercy of the LORD is from everlasting to
everlasting
On those who fear Him,
And His righteousness to children's children.

Psalm 103:13–17

We have sinned with our fathers,
We have committed iniquity,
We have done wickedly.
Our fathers in Egypt did not understand Your
wonders;

They did not remember the multitude of Your
mercies,
But rebelled by the sea—the Red Sea.
Nevertheless He saved them for His name's sake,
That He might make His mighty power known.

Psalm 106:6–8

Many times He delivered them;
But they rebelled in their counsel,
And were brought low for their iniquity.
Nevertheless He regarded their affliction,
When He heard their cry;
And for their sake He remembered His covenant,
And relented according to the multitude of His
mercies.

Psalm 106:43–45

Even a child is known by his deeds,
Whether what he does is pure and right.

Proverbs 20:11

The proverbs of Solomon:
A wise son makes a glad father,
But a foolish son is the grief of his mother.

Proverbs 10:1

"If you are willing and obedient,
You shall eat the good of the land;

"But if you refuse and rebel,
You shall be devoured by the sword";
For the mouth of the LORD has spoken.

Isaiah 1:19–20

Obey those who rule over you, and be submissive, for they watch out for your souls, as those who must give account. Let them do so with joy and not with grief, for that would be unprofitable for you.

Hebrews 13:17

So Samuel said:
"Has the LORD as great delight in burnt offerings and sacrifices,
As in obeying the voice of the LORD?
Behold, to obey is better than sacrifice,
And to heed than the fat of rams.
For rebellion is as the sin of witchcraft,
And stubbornness is as iniquity and idolatry.
Because you have rejected the word of the LORD,
He also has rejected you from being king."

1 Samuel 15:22–23

Foolishness is bound up in the heart of a child;
The rod of correction will drive it far from him.

Proverbs 22:15

A wise son heeds his father's instruction,
But a scoffer does not listen to rebuke.

Proverbs 13:1

Likewise you younger people, submit yourselves to your elders. Yes, all of you be submissive to one another, and be clothed with humility,
for "God resists the proud,
But gives grace to the humble."
Therefore humble yourselves under the mighty hand of God, that He may exalt you in due time.

I Peter 5:5–6

A member of your family dies

∞

He heals the brokenhearted
And binds up their wounds.
He counts the number of the stars;
He calls them all by name.
Great is our Lord, and mighty in power;
His understanding is infinite.

Psalm 147:3–5

But I do not want you to be ignorant, brethren, concerning those who have fallen asleep, lest you sorrow as others who have no hope.

For if we believe that Jesus died and rose again, even so God will bring with Him those who sleep in Jesus.

For this we say to you by the word of the Lord, that we who are alive and remain until the coming of the Lord will by no means precede those who are asleep.

For the Lord Himself will descend from heaven with a shout, with the voice of an archangel, and with the trumpet of God. And the dead in Christ will rise first.

I Thessalonians 4:13–16

For if the dead do not rise, then Christ is not risen.

And if Christ is not risen, your faith is futile; you are still in your sins!

Then also those who have fallen asleep in Christ have perished.

If in this life only we have hope in Christ, we are of all men the most pitiable.

But now Christ is risen from the dead, and has become the firstfruits of those who have fallen asleep.

For since by man came death, by Man also came the resurrection of the dead.

For as in Adam all die, even so in Christ all shall be made alive.

But each one in his own order: Christ the firstfruits, afterward those who are Christ's at His coming.

Then comes the end, when He delivers the kingdom to God the Father, when He puts an end to all rule and all authority and power.

For He must reign till He has put all enemies under His feet.

The last enemy that will be destroyed is death.

I Corinthians 15:16–26

Your kingdom is an everlasting kingdom, and Your dominion endures throughout all generations.

The LORD upholds all who fall, and raises up all who are bowed down.

Psalm 145:13–14

To everything there is a season,
A time for every purpose under heaven:
A time to be born,
And a time to die;
A time to plant,
And a time to pluck what is planted;
A time to kill,
And a time to heal;
A time to break down,
And a time to build up;
A time to weep,
And a time to laugh;
A time to mourn,
And a time to dance;
A time to cast away stones,
And a time to gather stones;
A time to embrace,
And a time to refrain from embracing;
A time to gain,
And a time to lose;
A time to keep,
And a time to throw away;
A time to tear,

And a time to sew;
A time to keep silence,
And a time to speak;
A time to love,
And a time to hate;
A time of war,
And a time of peace.

Ecclesiastes 3:1–8

Anger threatens
your home's peace

∞

Behold, how good and how pleasant it is
For brethren to dwell together in unity!
It is like the precious oil upon the head,
Running down on the beard,
The beard of Aaron,
Running down on the edge of his garments.

Psalm 133:1–2

He who is slow to wrath has great understanding,
But he who is impulsive exalts folly.

Proverbs 14:29

Better is a dinner of herbs where love is,
Than a fatted calf with hatred.
A wrathful man stirs up strife,
But he who is slow to anger allays contention.

Proverbs 15:17–18

I am for peace;
But when I speak, they are for war.
I will lift up my eyes to the hills—

From whence comes my help?
My help comes from the LORD,
Who made heaven and earth.
He will not allow your foot to be moved;
He who keeps you will not slumber.

Psalm 120:7; 121:1–3

He who is slow to anger is better than the mighty,
And he who rules his spirit than he who takes a city.

Proverbs 16:32

The beginning of strife is like releasing water;
Therefore stop contention before a quarrel starts.

Proverbs 17:14

For God is not the author of confusion but of peace, as in all the churches of the saints.

I Corinthians 14:33

So then, my beloved brethren, let every man be swift to hear, slow to speak, slow to wrath;
for the wrath of man does not produce the righteousness of God.

James 1:19–20

"Be angry, and do not sin": do not let the sun go down on your wrath.

Ephesians 4:26

Hear my prayer, O LORD,
And let my cry come to You.
Do not hide Your face from me in the day of my trouble;
Incline Your ear to me;
In the day that I call, answer me speedily.
For my days are consumed like smoke,
And my bones are burned like a hearth.
My heart is stricken and withered like grass,
So that I forget to eat my bread.

Psalm 102:1–4

But You, O LORD, shall endure forever,
And the remembrance of Your name to all generations.

Psalm 102:12

Let your speech always be with grace, seasoned with salt, that you may know how you ought to answer each one.

Colossians 4:6

Whoever guards his mouth and tongue
Keeps his soul from troubles.

Proverbs 21:23

Pleasant words are like a honeycomb,
Sweetness to the soul and health to the bones.

Proverbs 16:24

Now I plead with you, brethren, by the name of our Lord Jesus Christ, that you all speak the same thing, and that there be no divisions among you, but that you be perfectly joined together in the same mind and in the same judgment.

I Corinthians 1:10

Your family grows apart

∞

God sets the solitary in families;
He brings out those who are bound into prosperity;
But the rebellious dwell in a dry land.

Psalm 68:6

Children's children are the crown of old men,
And the glory of children is their father.

Proverbs 17:6

Therefore my spirit is overwhelmed within me;
My heart within me is distressed.
I remember the days of old;
I meditate on all Your works;
I muse on the work of Your hands.
I spread out my hands to You;
My soul longs for You like a thirsty land. Selah
Answer me speedily, O LORD;
My spirit fails! Do not hide Your face from me,
Lest I be like those who go down into the pit.
Cause me to hear Your lovingkindness in the
morning,
For in You do I trust;

Cause me to know the way in which I should walk,
For I lift up my soul to You.

Psalm 143:4–8

He who heeds the word wisely will find good,
And whoever trusts in the LORD, happy is he.

Proverbs 16:20

A merry heart makes a cheerful countenance,
But by sorrow of the heart the spirit is broken.
The heart of him who has understanding seeks
knowledge,
But the mouth of fools feeds on foolishness.
All the days of the afflicted are evil,
But he who is of a merry heart has a continual feast.
Better is a little with the fear of the LORD,
Than great treasure with trouble.

Proverbs 15:13–16

The wise woman builds her house,
But the foolish pulls it down with her hands.

Proverbs 14:1

And I, brethren, could not speak to you as to spiritual
people but as to carnal, as to babes in Christ.

I fed you with milk and not with solid food; for
until now you were not able to receive it, and even now
you are still not able;

for you are still carnal. For where there are envy, strife, and divisions among you, are you not carnal and behaving like mere men?

I Corinthians 3:1–3

For by one Spirit we were all baptized into one body—whether Jews or Greeks, whether slaves or free—and have all been made to drink into one Spirit.

For in fact the body is not one member but many.

If the foot should say, "Because I am not a hand, I am not of the body," is it therefore not of the body?

And if the ear should say, "Because I am not an eye, I am not of the body," is it therefore not of the body?

If the whole body were an eye, where would be the hearing? If the whole were hearing, where would be the smelling?

But now God has set the members, each one of them, in the body just as He pleased.

And if they were all one member, where would the body be?

But now indeed there are many members, yet one body.

And the eye cannot say to the hand, "I have no need of you"; nor again the head to the feet, "I have no need of you."

No, much rather, those members of the body which seem to be weaker are necessary.

And those members of the body which we think to be less honorable, on these we bestow greater honor; and our unpresentable parts have greater modesty,

but our presentable parts have no need. But God composed the body, having given greater honor to that part which lacks it,

that there should be no schism in the body, but that the members should have the same care for one another.

And if one member suffers, all the members suffer with it; or if one member is honored, all the members rejoice with it.

I Corinthians 12:13–26

But Jesus knew their thoughts, and said to them: "Every kingdom divided against itself is brought to desolation, and every city or house divided against itself will not stand."

Matthew 12:25

A brother offended is harder to win than a strong city,
And contentions are like the bars of a castle.

Proverbs 18:19

A merry heart does good, like medicine,
But a broken spirit dries the bones.

Proverbs 17:22

Better is a dry morsel with quietness,
Than a house full of feasting with strife.

Proverbs 17:1

Pursue peace with all people, and holiness, without which no one will see the Lord:

looking carefully lest anyone fall short of the grace of God; lest any root of bitterness springing up cause trouble, and by this many become defiled.

Hebrews 12:14–15

GOD PROTECTS
YOU WHEN

You are concerned about the world's influence on your children

∞

My son, keep your father's command,
And do not forsake the law of your mother.
Bind them continually upon your heart;
Tie them around your neck.
When you roam, they will lead you;
When you sleep, they will keep you;
And when you awake, they will speak with you.
For the commandment is a lamp,
And the law a light;
Reproofs of instruction are the way of life.

Proverbs 6:20–23

Train up a child in the way he should go,
And when he is old he will not depart from it.

Proverbs 22:6

Whoever keeps the law is a discerning son,
But a companion of gluttons shames his father.

Proverbs 28:7

When He had called the people to Himself, with His disciples also, He said to them, "Whoever desires to come after Me, let him deny himself, and take up his cross, and follow Me.

"For whoever desires to save his life will lose it, but whoever loses his life for My sake and the gospel's will save it.

"For what will it profit a man if he gains the whole world, and loses his own soul?"

Mark 8:34–36

I beseech you therefore, brethren, by the mercies of God, that you present your bodies a living sacrifice, holy, acceptable to God, which is your reasonable service.

And do not be conformed to this world, but be transformed by the renewing of your mind, that you may prove what is that good and acceptable and perfect will of God.

Romans 12:1–2

Do not be unequally yoked together with unbelievers. For what fellowship has righteousness with lawlessness? And what communion has light with darkness?

And what accord has Christ with Belial? Or what part has a believer with an unbeliever?

And what agreement has the temple of God with idols? For you are the temple of the living God. As God has said:

*"I will dwell in them
And walk among them.
I will be their God,
And they shall be My people."*

Therefore *"Come out from among them and be separate, says the Lord. Do not touch what is unclean, and I will receive you."*

"I will be a Father to you, and you shall be My sons and daughters, says the LORD Almighty."

II Corinthians 6:14–18

For the unbelieving husband is sanctified by the wife, and the unbelieving wife is sanctified by the husband; otherwise your children would be unclean, but now they are holy.

I Corinthians 7:14

Deliver yourself like a gazelle from the hand of
the hunter,
And like a bird from the hand of the fowler.
Go to the ant, you sluggard!
Consider her ways and be wise,
Which, having no captain,
Overseer or ruler,
Provides her supplies in the summer,
And gathers her food in the harvest.
How long will you slumber, O sluggard?
When will you rise from your sleep?

A little sleep, a little slumber,
A little folding of the hands to sleep—
So shall your poverty come on you like a prowler,
And your need like an armed man.

Proverbs 6:5–11

Let no one deceive you with empty words, for because of these things the wrath of God comes upon the sons of disobedience.

Therefore do not be partakers with them.

For you were once darkness, but now you are light in the Lord. Walk as children of light

(for the fruit of the Spirit is in all goodness, righteousness, and truth),

finding out what is acceptable to the Lord.

And have no fellowship with the unfruitful works of darkness, but rather expose them.

For it is shameful even to speak of those things which are done by them in secret.

Ephesians 5:6–12

"Beware of false prophets, who come to you in sheep's clothing, but inwardly they are ravenous wolves.

"You will know them by their fruits. Do men gather grapes from thornbushes or figs from thistles?

"Even so, every good tree bears good fruit, but a bad tree bears bad fruit."

Matthew 7:15–17

So shall My word be that goes forth from My mouth;
It shall not return to Me void,
But it shall accomplish what I please,
And it shall prosper in the thing for which I sent it.
For you shall go out with joy,
And be led out with peace;
The mountains and the hills
Shall break forth into singing before you,
And all the trees of the field shall clap their hands.
Instead of the thorn shall come up the cypress tree,
And instead of the brier shall come up the myrtle
tree;
And it shall be to the LORD for a name,
For an everlasting sign that shall not be cut off.

Isaiah 55:11–13

No temptation has overtaken you except such as is common to man; but God is faithful, who will not allow you to be tempted beyond what you are able, but with the temptation will also make the way of escape, that you may be able to bear it.

I Corinthians 10:13

You don't know what decisions are best for your family

∞

The steps of a good man are ordered by the LORD,
And He delights in his way.
Though he fall, he shall not be utterly cast down;
For the LORD upholds him with His hand.

Psalm 37:23–24

All your children shall be taught by the LORD,
And great shall be the peace of your children.

Isaiah 54:13

And though the Lord gives you
The bread of adversity and the water of affliction,
Yet your teachers will not be moved into a corner anymore,
But your eyes shall see your teachers.
Your ears shall hear a word behind you, saying,
"This is the way, walk in it,"
Whenever you turn to the right hand
Or whenever you turn to the left.

Isaiah 30:20–21

Incline your ear and hear the words of the wise,
And apply your heart to my knowledge;
For it is a pleasant thing if you keep them within
you;
Let them all be fixed upon your lips.

Proverbs 22:17–18

"Now therefore, fear the LORD, serve Him in sincerity and in truth, and put away the gods which your fathers served on the other side of the River and in Egypt. Serve the LORD!

"And if it seems evil to you to serve the LORD, choose for yourselves this day whom you will serve, whether the gods which your fathers served that were on the other side of the River, or the gods of the Amorites, in whose land you dwell. But as for me and my house, we will serve the LORD."

So the people answered and said: "Far be it from us that we should forsake the LORD to serve other gods."

Joshua 24:14–16

The LORD will guide you continually,
And satisfy your soul in drought,
And strengthen your bones;
You shall be like a watered garden,
And like a spring of water, whose waters do not fail.
Those from among you

Shall build the old waste places;
You shall raise up the foundations of many
generations;
And you shall be called the Repairer of the Breach,
The Restorer of Streets to Dwell In.

Isaiah 58:11–12

You have dealt well with Your servant,
O LORD, according to Your word.
Teach me good judgment and knowledge,
For I believe Your commandments.

Psalm 119:65–66

I was so foolish and ignorant;
I was like a beast before You.
Nevertheless I am continually with You;
You hold me by my right hand.
You will guide me with Your counsel,
And afterward receive me to glory.
Whom have I in heaven but You?
And there is none upon earth that I desire besides
You.
My flesh and my heart fail;
But God is the strength of my heart and my
portion forever.

Psalm 73:22–26

You also gave Your good Spirit to instruct them,
And did not withhold Your manna from their mouth,
And gave them water for their thirst.

Nehemiah 9:20

Do all things without complaining and disputing,
that you may become blameless and harmless, children of God without fault in the midst of a crooked and
perverse generation, among whom you shine as lights in
the world,
holding fast the word of life, so that I may rejoice in
the day of Christ that I have not run in vain or labored
in vain.

Philippians 2:14–16

Trust in the LORD with all your heart,
And lean not on your own understanding;
In all your ways acknowledge Him,
And He shall direct your paths.

Proverbs 3:5–6

"Listen to Me, O Jacob,
And Israel, My called:
I am He, I am the First,
I am also the Last.
Indeed My hand has laid the foundation of the
earth,

And My right hand has stretched out the heavens;
When I call to them,
They stand up together.
Come near to Me, hear this:
I have not spoken in secret from the beginning;
From the time that it was, I was there.
And now the Lord GOD and His Spirit
Have sent Me."
Thus says the LORD, your Redeemer,
The Holy One of Israel:
"I am the LORD your God,
Who teaches you to profit,
Who leads you by the way you should go."

Isaiah 48:12–13, 16–17

You question God's power
to meet all situations

∞

Behold, happy is the man whom God corrects;
Therefore do not despise the chastening of the
Almighty.
For He bruises, but He binds up;
He wounds, but His hands make whole.
He shall deliver you in six troubles,
Yes, in seven no evil shall touch you.
In famine He shall redeem you from death,
And in war from the power of the sword.
You shall be hidden from the scourge of the tongue,
And you shall not be afraid of destruction when it
comes.
You shall laugh at destruction and famine,
And you shall not be afraid of the beasts of the earth.
For you shall have a covenant with the stones of the
field,
And the beasts of the field shall be at peace with you.
You shall know that your tent is in peace;
You shall visit your dwelling and find nothing amiss.
You shall also know that your descendants shall
be many,

And your offspring like the grass of the earth.
You shall come to the grave at a full age,
As a sheaf of grain ripens in its season.
Behold, this we have searched out;
It is true.
Hear it, and know for yourself.

Job 5:17–27

For our gospel did not come to you in word only, but also in power, and in the Holy Spirit and in much assurance, as you know what kind of men we were among you for your sake.

I Thessalonians 1:5

Now may the God of peace Himself sanctify you completely; and may your whole spirit, soul, and body be preserved blameless at the coming of our Lord Jesus Christ.

He who calls you is faithful, who also will do it.

I Thessalonians 5:23–24

For this reason we also, since the day we heard it, do not cease to pray for you, and to ask that you may be filled with the knowledge of His will in all wisdom and spiritual understanding;

that you may walk worthy of the Lord, fully pleasing Him, being fruitful in every good work and increasing in the knowledge of God;

strengthened with all might, according to His glorious power, for all patience and longsuffering with joy;

giving thanks to the Father who has qualified us to be partakers of the inheritance of the saints in the light.

He has delivered us from the power of darkness and conveyed us into the kingdom of the Son of His love.

Colossians 1:9–13

And the apostles said to the Lord, "Increase our faith."

So the Lord said, "If you have faith as a mustard seed, you can say to this mulberry tree, 'Be pulled up by the roots and be planted in the sea,' and it would obey you."

Luke 17:5–6

Now when He got into a boat, His disciples followed Him.

And suddenly a great tempest arose on the sea, so that the boat was covered with the waves. But He was asleep.

Then His disciples came to Him and awoke Him, saying, "Lord, save us! We are perishing!"

But He said to them, "Why are you fearful, O you of little faith?" Then He arose and rebuked the winds and the sea, and there was a great calm.

So the men marveled, saying, "Who can this be, that even the winds and the sea obey Him?"

Matthew 8:23–27

Therefore I also, after I heard of your faith in the Lord Jesus and your love for all the saints,

do not cease to give thanks for you, making mention of you in my prayers:

that the God of our Lord Jesus Christ, the Father of glory, may give to you the spirit of wisdom and revelation in the knowledge of Him,

the eyes of your understanding being enlightened; that you may know what is the hope of His calling, what are the riches of the glory of His inheritance in the saints,

and what is the exceeding greatness of His power toward us who believe, according to the working of His mighty power

which He worked in Christ when He raised Him from the dead and seated Him at His right hand in the heavenly places,

far above all principality and power and might and dominion, and every name that is named, not only in this age but also in that which is to come.

And He put all things under His feet, and gave Him to be head over all things to the church,

which is His body, the fullness of Him who fills all in all.

Ephesians 1:15–23

You feel depressed and
lose your way

∞

Now faith is the substance of things hoped for, the evidence of things not seen.

For by it the elders obtained a good testimony.

By faith we understand that the worlds were framed by the word of God, so that the things which are seen were not made of things which are visible.

These all died in faith, not having received the promises, but having seen them afar off were assured of them, embraced them and confessed that they were strangers and pilgrims on the earth.

Hebrews 11:1–3, 13

Then the Lord knows how to deliver the godly out of temptations and to reserve the unjust under punishment for the day of judgment.

II Peter 2:9

For you have need of endurance, so that after you have done the will of God, you may receive the promise:

"For yet a little while,
And He who is coming will come and will not tarry."

Hebrews 10:36–37

You have not yet resisted to bloodshed, striving against sin.

And you have forgotten the exhortation which speaks to you as to sons:

"My son, do not despise the chastening of the LORD,
Nor be discouraged when you are rebuked by Him;
"For whom the LORD loves He chastens,
And scourges every son whom He receives."

Hebrews 12:4–6

Whoever seeks to save his life will lose it, and whoever loses his life will preserve it.

Luke 17:33

Nevertheless He saved them for His name's sake,
That He might make His mighty power known.

Psalm 106:8

So we may boldly say:
"The LORD is my helper;
I will not fear.
What can man do to me?"

Hebrews 13:6

Therefore submit to God. Resist the devil and he will flee from you.

Draw near to God and He will draw near to you.

Cleanse your hands, you sinners; and purify your hearts, you double-minded.

Lament and mourn and weep! Let your laughter be turned to mourning and your joy to gloom.

Humble yourselves in the sight of the Lord, and He will lift you up.

James 4:7–10

Blessed is the man who endures temptation; for when he has been approved, he will receive the crown of life which the Lord has promised to those who love Him.

Let no one say when he is tempted, "I am tempted by God"; for God cannot be tempted by evil, nor does He Himself tempt anyone.

But each one is tempted when he is drawn away by his own desires and enticed.

Then, when desire has conceived, it gives birth to sin; and sin, when it is full-grown, brings forth death.

Do not be deceived, my beloved brethren.

James 1:12–16

Yet if anyone suffers as a Christian, let him not be ashamed, but let him glorify God in this matter.

Therefore let those who suffer according to the will of God commit their souls to Him in doing good, as to a faithful Creator.

I Peter 4:16, 19

Having a good conscience, that when they defame you as evildoers, those who revile your good conduct in Christ may be ashamed.

For it is better, if it is the will of God, to suffer for doing good than for doing evil.

For Christ also suffered once for sins, the just for the unjust, that He might bring us to God, being put to death in the flesh but made alive by the Spirit.

I Peter 3:16–18

My little children, these things I write to you, so that you may not sin. And if anyone sins, we have an Advocate with the Father, Jesus Christ the righteous.

And He Himself is the propitiation for our sins, and not for ours only but also for the whole world.

1 John 2:1–2

GOD CHALLENGES
YOU TO

Teach your children to love God

∞

I write to you, little children,
Because your sins are forgiven you for His name's sake.
I write to you, fathers,
Because you have known Him who is from the beginning.
I write to you, young men,
Because you have overcome the wicked one.
I write to you, little children,
Because you have known the Father.
I have written to you, fathers,
Because you have known Him who is from the beginning.
I have written to you, young men,
Because you are strong, and the word of God abides in you,
And you have overcome the wicked one.

Do not love the world or the things in the world. If anyone loves the world, the love of the Father is not in him.

For all that is in the world—the lust of the flesh,

the lust of the eyes, and the pride of life—is not of the Father but is of the world.

And the world is passing away, and the lust of it; but he who does the will of God abides forever.

I John 2:12–17

Beloved, let us love one another, for love is of God; and everyone who loves is born of God and knows God.

He who does not love does not know God, for God is love.

In this the love of God was manifested toward us, that God has sent His only begotten Son into the world, that we might live through Him.

In this is love, not that we loved God, but that He loved us and sent His Son to be the propitiation for our sins.

Beloved, if God so loved us, we also ought to love one another.

No one has seen God at any time. If we love one another, God abides in us, and His love has been perfected in us.

By this we know that we abide in Him, and He in us, because He has given us of His Spirit.

And we have seen and testify that the Father has sent the Son as Savior of the world.

Whoever confesses that Jesus is the Son of God, God abides in him, and he in God.

And we have known and believed the love that God has for us. God is love, and he who abides in love abides in God, and God in him.

Love has been perfected among us in this: that we may have boldness in the day of judgment; because as He is, so are we in this world.

There is no fear in love; but perfect love casts out fear, because fear involves torment. But he who fears has not been made perfect in love.

We love Him because He first loved us.

If someone says, "I love God," and hates his brother, he is a liar; for he who does not love his brother whom he has seen, how can he love God whom he has not seen?

And this commandment we have from Him: that he who loves God must love his brother also.

I John 4:7–21

Then little children were brought to Him that He might put His hands on them and pray, but the disciples rebuked them.

But Jesus said, "Let the little children come to Me, and do not forbid them; for of such is the kingdom of heaven."

And He laid His hands on them and departed from there.

Matthew 19:13–15

He came to His own, and His own did not receive Him.

But as many as received Him, to them He gave the right to become children of God, to those who believe in His name.

John 1:11–12

Jesus answered and said to him, "Most assuredly, I say to you, unless one is born again, he cannot see the kingdom of God."

Nicodemus said to Him, "How can a man be born when he is old? Can he enter a second time into his mother's womb and be born?"

Jesus answered, "Most assuredly, I say to you, unless one is born of water and the Spirit, he cannot enter the kingdom of God.

That which is born of the flesh is flesh, and that which is born of the Spirit is spirit.

Do not marvel that I said to you, 'You must be born again.'"

John 3:3–7

Grow in your own
Christian walk
∞

The Elder, To the beloved Gaius, whom I love in truth: Beloved, I pray that you may prosper in all things and be in health, just as your soul prospers.

For I rejoiced greatly when brethren came and testified of the truth that is in you, just as you walk in the truth.

I have no greater joy than to hear that my children walk in truth.

III John 1–4

Teach me, O LORD, the way of Your statutes,
And I shall keep it to the end.
Give me understanding, and I shall keep Your law;
Indeed, I shall observe it with my whole heart.
Make me walk in the path of Your commandments,
For I delight in it.

Psalm 119:33–35

Now by this we know that we know Him, if we keep His commandments.

He who says, "I know Him," and does not keep His commandments, is a liar, and the truth is not in him.

But whoever keeps His word, truly the love of God is perfected in him. By this we know that we are in Him.

He who says he abides in Him ought himself also to walk just as He walked.

I John 2:3–6

Your word is a lamp to my feet
And a light to my path.
I have sworn and confirmed
That I will keep Your righteous judgments.
I am afflicted very much;
Revive me, O LORD, according to Your word.
Accept, I pray, the freewill offerings of my mouth,
O LORD,
And teach me Your judgments.
My life is continually in my hand,
Yet I do not forget Your law.

Psalm 119:105–109

Therefore, having these promises, beloved, let us cleanse ourselves from all filthiness of the flesh and spirit, perfecting holiness in the fear of God.

II Corinthians 7:1

Apply your heart to instruction,
And your ears to words of knowledge.

Proverbs 23:12

Teach me Your way, O LORD;
I will walk in Your truth;
Unite my heart to fear Your name.
I will praise You, O Lord my God, with all my heart,
And I will glorify Your name forevermore.

Psalm 86:11–12

Because it is written, *"Be holy, for I am holy."*

I Peter 1:16

You cannot drink the cup of the Lord and the cup of demons; you cannot partake of the Lord's table and of the table of demons.

Or do we provoke the Lord to jealousy? Are we stronger than He?

All things are lawful for me, but not all things are helpful; all things are lawful for me, but not all things edify.

I Corinthians 10:21–23

That the righteous requirement of the law might be fulfilled in us who do not walk according to the flesh but according to the Spirit.

For those who live according to the flesh set their minds on the things of the flesh, but those who live according to the Spirit, the things of the Spirit.

For to be carnally minded is death, but to be spiritually minded is life and peace.

Romans 8:4–6

Two men went up to the temple to pray, one a Pharisee and the other a tax collector.

The Pharisee stood and prayed thus with himself, "God, I thank You that I am not like other men—extortioners, unjust, adulterers, or even as this tax collector.

"I fast twice a week; I give tithes of all that I possess."

And the tax collector, standing afar off, would not so much as raise his eyes to heaven, but beat his breast, saying, "God, be merciful to me a sinner!"

I tell you, this man went down to his house justified rather than the other; for everyone who exalts himself will be humbled, and he who humbles himself will be exalted.

Luke 18:10–14

And do this, knowing the time, that now it is high time to awake out of sleep; for now our salvation is nearer than when we first believed.

The night is far spent, the day is at hand. Therefore let us cast off the works of darkness, and let us put on the armor of light.

Let us walk properly, as in the day, not in revelry and drunkenness, not in lewdness and lust, not in strife and envy.

But put on the Lord Jesus Christ, and make no provision for the flesh, to fulfill its lusts.

Romans 13:11–14

Fight the good fight of faith, lay hold on eternal life, to which you were also called and have confessed the good confession in the presence of many witnesses.

I Timothy 6:12

Whoever believes that Jesus is the Christ is born of God, and everyone who loves Him who begot also loves him who is begotten of Him.

By this we know that we love the children of God, when we love God and keep His commandments.

For this is the love of God, that we keep His commandments. And His commandments are not burdensome.

I John 5:1–3

Share your faith
with your children

∞

Then Jesus called a little child to Him, set him in the midst of them,

and said, "Assuredly, I say to you, unless you are converted and become as little children, you will by no means enter the kingdom of heaven.

"Therefore whoever humbles himself as this little child is the greatest in the kingdom of heaven.

"Whoever receives one little child like this in My name receives Me.

"Whoever causes one of these little ones who believe in Me to sin, it would be better for him if a millstone were hung around his neck, and he were drowned in the depth of the sea.

"Take heed that you do not despise one of these little ones, for I say to you that in heaven their angels always see the face of My Father who is in heaven.

"For the Son of Man has come to save that which was lost.

"What do you think? If a man has a hundred sheep, and one of them goes astray, does he not leave the ninety-nine and go to the mountains to seek the one that is straying?

"And if he should find it, assuredly, I say to you, he rejoices more over that sheep than over the ninety-nine that did not go astray.

"Even so it is not the will of your Father who is in heaven that one of these little ones should perish."

Matthew 18:2–6, 10–14

And these words which I command you today shall be in your heart.

You shall teach them diligently to your children, and shall talk of them when you sit in your house, when you walk by the way, when you lie down, and when you rise up.

You shall bind them as a sign on your hand, and they shall be as frontlets between your eyes.

You shall write them on the doorposts of your house and on your gates.

Deuteronomy 6:6–9

But before faith came, we were kept under guard by the law, kept for the faith which would afterward be revealed.

Therefore the law was our tutor to bring us to Christ, that we might be justified by faith.

But after faith has come, we are no longer under a tutor.

For you are all sons of God through faith in Christ
Jesus.

For as many of you as were baptized into Christ have
put on Christ.

Galatians 3:23–27

But what does it say? *"The word is near you, in your
mouth and in your heart"* (that is, the word of faith which
we preach):

that if you confess with your mouth the Lord Jesus
and believe in your heart that God has raised Him from
the dead, you will be saved.

For with the heart one believes unto righteousness,
and with the mouth confession is made unto salvation.

For the Scripture says, *"Whoever believes on Him will
not be put to shame."*

Romans 10:8–11

For this is good and acceptable in the sight of God
our Savior,

Who desires all men to be saved and to come to the
knowledge of the truth.

I Timothy 2:3–4

Brethren, if anyone among you wanders from the
truth, and someone turns him back,

let him know that he who turns a sinner from the

error of his way will save a soul from death and cover a multitude of sins.

James 5:19–20

For the equipping of the saints for the work of ministry, for the edifying of the body of Christ,

till we all come to the unity of the faith and of the knowledge of the Son of God, to a perfect man, to the measure of the stature of the fullness of Christ;

that we should no longer be children, tossed to and fro and carried about with every wind of doctrine, by the trickery of men, in the cunning craftiness of deceitful plotting,

but, speaking the truth in love, may grow up in all things into Him who is the head—Christ.

Ephesians 4:12–15

And the keeper of the prison, awaking from sleep and seeing the prison doors open, supposing the prisoners had fled, drew his sword and was about to kill himself.

But Paul called with a loud voice, saying, "Do yourself no harm, for we are all here."

Then he called for a light, ran in, and fell down trembling before Paul and Silas.

And he brought them out and said, "Sirs, what must I do to be saved?"

So they said, "Believe on the Lord Jesus Christ, and you will be saved, you and your household."

Then they spoke the word of the Lord to him and to all who were in his house.

And he took them the same hour of the night and washed their stripes. And immediately he and all his family were baptized.

Acts 16:27–33

Then they brought little children to Him, that He might touch them; but the disciples rebuked those who brought them.

But when Jesus saw it, He was greatly displeased and said to them, "Let the little children come to Me, and do not forbid them; for of such is the kingdom of God.

"Assuredly, I say to you, whoever does not receive the kingdom of God as a little child will by no means enter it."

And He took them up in His arms, laid His hands on them, and blessed them.

Mark 10:13–16

Deal honestly with those close to you

∞

The fathers have eaten sour grapes,
And the children's teeth are set on edge.

Jeremiah 31:29b

Judge not, that you be not judged.

For with what judgment you judge, you will be judged; and with the measure you use, it will be measured back to you.

And why do you look at the speck in your brother's eye, but do not consider the plank in your own eye?

Or how can you say to your brother, "Let me remove the speck from your eye"; and look, a plank is in your own eye?

Hypocrite! First remove the plank from your own eye, and then you will see clearly to remove the speck from your brother's eye.

Matthew 7:1–5

Do not lie to one another, since you have put off the old man with his deeds,

and have put on the new man who is renewed in

knowledge according to the image of Him who created him.

Colossians 3:9–10

Do not withhold good from those to whom it is due,
When it is in the power of your hand to do so.

Proverbs 3:27

He who is often rebuked, and hardens his neck,
Will suddenly be destroyed, and that without remedy.

Proverbs 29:1

Lying lips are an abomination to the LORD,
But those who deal truthfully are His delight.

Proverbs 12:22

Then the LORD sent Nathan to David. And he came to him, and said to him: "There were two men in one city, one rich and the other poor.

"The rich man had exceedingly many flocks and herds.

"But the poor man had nothing, except one little ewe lamb which he had bought and nourished; and it grew up together with him and with his children. It ate of his own food and drank from his own cup and lay in his bosom; and it was like a daughter to him.

"And a traveler came to the rich man, who refused

to take from his own flock and from his own herd to prepare one for the wayfaring man who had come to him;
but he took the poor man's lamb and prepared it for the
man who had come to him."

So David's anger was greatly aroused against the
man, and he said to Nathan, "As the LORD lives, the
man who has done this shall surely die!

"And he shall restore fourfold for the lamb, because
he did this thing and because he had no pity."

Then Nathan said to David, "You are the man!"

II Samuel 12:1–7a

And take not the word of truth utterly out of my
    mouth,
For I have hoped in Your ordinances.
So shall I keep Your law continually,
Forever and ever.
And I will walk at liberty,
For I seek Your precepts.

Psalm 119:43–45

If indeed you have heard Him and have been taught
by Him, as the truth is in Jesus:

that you put off, concerning your former conduct,
the old man which grows corrupt according to the deceitful lusts,

and be renewed in the spirit of your mind,

and that you put on the new man which was created according to God, in true righteousness and holiness.

Therefore, putting away lying, *"Let each one of you speak truth with his neighbor,"* for we are members of one another.

Ephesians 4:21–25

Ask forgiveness when you wrong your family

∞

And he will turn
The hearts of the fathers to the children,
And the hearts of the children to their fathers,
Lest I come and strike the earth with a curse.

Malachi 4:6

He who covers his sins will not prosper,
But whoever confesses and forsakes them will have
mercy.

Proverbs 28:13

A man's pride will bring him low,
But the humble in spirit will retain honor.

Proverbs 29:23

Take heed to yourselves. If your brother sins against
you, rebuke him; and if he repents, forgive him.
And if he sins against you seven times in a day, and
seven times in a day returns to you, saying, "I repent," you
shall forgive him.

Luke 17:3–4

And whenever you stand praying, if you have anything against anyone, forgive him, that your Father in heaven may also forgive you your trespasses.

But if you do not forgive, neither will your Father in heaven forgive your trespasses.

Mark 11:25–26

The righteous man walks in his integrity;
His children are blessed after him.

Proverbs 20:7

I, therefore, the prisoner of the Lord, beseech you to walk worthy of the calling with which you were called,

with all lowliness and gentleness, with longsuffering, bearing with one another in love,

endeavoring to keep the unity of the Spirit in the bond of peace.

Ephesians 4:1–3

Bearing with one another, and forgiving one another, if anyone has a complaint against another; even as Christ forgave you, so you also must do.

Colossians 3:13

For if you forgive men their trespasses, your heavenly Father will also forgive you.

But if you do not forgive men their trespasses, neither will your Father forgive your trespasses.

Matthew 6:14–15

Never stop loving your wife

∞

Live joyfully with the wife whom you love all the days of your vain life which He has given you under the sun, all your days of vanity; for that is your portion in life, and in the labor which you perform under the sun.

Ecclesiastes 9:9

Many waters cannot quench love,
Nor can the floods drown it.
If a man would give for love
All the wealth of his house,
It would be utterly despised.

Song of Solomon 8:7

He who finds a wife finds a good thing,
And obtains favor from the LORD.

Proverbs 18:22

Who satisfies your mouth with good things,
So that your youth is renewed like the eagle's.

Psalm 103:5

Let your fountain be blessed,
And rejoice with the wife of your youth.

As a loving deer and a graceful doe,
Let her breasts satisfy you at all times;
And always be enraptured with her love.

Proverbs 5:18–19

And He answered and said to them, "Have you not read that He who made them at the beginning *'made them male and female,'*

"and said, *'For this reason a man shall leave his father and mother and be joined to his wife, and the two shall become one flesh'*?

"So then, they are no longer two but one flesh. Therefore what God has joined together, let not man separate."

Matthew 19:4–6

How fair is your love,
My sister, my spouse!
How much better than wine is your love,
And the scent of your perfumes than all spices!
Your lips, O my spouse,
Drip as the honeycomb;
Honey and milk are under your tongue;
And the fragrance of your garments
Is like the fragrance of Lebanon.
A garden enclosed
Is my sister, my spouse,
A spring shut up,

A fountain sealed.
Your plants are an orchard of pomegranates
With pleasant fruits,
Fragrant henna with spikenard,
Spikenard and saffron,
Calamus and cinnamon,
With all trees of frankincense,
Myrrh and aloes,
With all the chief spices—
A fountain of gardens,
A well of living waters,
And streams from Lebanon.
Awake, O north wind,
And come, O south!
Blow upon my garden,
That its spices may flow out.
Let my beloved come to his garden
And eat its pleasant fruits.

Song of Solomon 4:10–16

And the LORD God said, "It is not good that man should be alone; I will make him a helper comparable to him."

Genesis 2:18

But from the beginning of the creation, God *"made them male and female.*

"*For this reason a man shall leave his father and mother and be joined to his wife,*

"*And the two shall become one flesh*"; so then they are no longer two, but one flesh.

Therefore what God has joined together, let not man separate.

Mark 10:6–9

Nevertheless, because of sexual immorality, let each man have his own wife, and let each woman have her own husband.

Let the husband render to his wife the affection due her, and likewise also the wife to her husband.

The wife does not have authority over her own body, but the husband does. And likewise the husband does not have authority over his own body, but the wife does.

Do not deprive one another except with consent for a time, that you may give yourselves to fasting and prayer; and come together again so that Satan does not tempt you because of your lack of self-control.

But I say this as a concession, not as a commandment.

I Corinthians 7:2–6

Marriage is honorable among all, and the bed undefiled; but fornicators and adulterers God will judge.

Hebrews 13:4

And the LORD God caused a deep sleep to fall on

Adam, and he slept; and He took one of his ribs, and closed up the flesh in its place.

Then the rib which the LORD God had taken from man He made into a woman, and He brought her to the man.

And Adam said:

"This is now bone of my bones
And flesh of my flesh;
She shall be called Woman,
Because she was taken out of Man."

Therefore a man shall leave his father and mother and be joined to his wife, and they shall become one flesh.

And they were both naked, the man and his wife, and were not ashamed.

Genesis 2:21–25

Houses and riches are an inheritance from fathers,
But a prudent wife is from the LORD.

Proverbs 19:14

Be wise with your family's finances

∞

Now it shall come to pass, if you diligently obey the voice of the LORD your God, to observe carefully all His commandments which I command you today, that the LORD your God will set you high above all nations of the earth.

And all these blessings shall come upon you and overtake you, because you obey the voice of the LORD your God:

Blessed shall you be in the city, and blessed shall you be in the country.

Blessed shall be the fruit of your body, the produce of your ground and the increase of your herds, the increase of your cattle and the offspring of your flocks.

Blessed shall be your basket and your kneading bowl.

Blessed shall you be when you come in, and blessed shall you be when you go out.

Deuteronomy 28:1–6

But if anyone does not provide for his own, and especially for those of his household, he has denied the faith and is worse than an unbeliever.

I Timothy 5:8

And you shall remember the LORD your God, for it is He who gives you power to get wealth, that He may establish His covenant which He swore to your fathers, as it is this day.

Deuteronomy 8:18

If they obey and serve Him,
They shall spend their days in prosperity,
And their years in pleasures.

Job 36:11

Trust in the LORD, and do good;
Dwell in the land, and feed on His faithfulness.
Delight yourself also in the LORD,
And He shall give you the desires of your heart.
Commit your way to the LORD,
Trust also in Him,
And He shall bring it to pass.

Psalm 37:3–5

Behold, My Servant shall deal prudently;
He shall be exalted and extolled and be very high.

Isaiah 52:13

I went by the field of the lazy man,
And by the vineyard of the man devoid of
understanding;
And there it was, all overgrown with thorns;
Its surface was covered with nettles;
Its stone wall was broken down.
When I saw it, I considered it well;
I looked on it and received instruction:
A little sleep, a little slumber,
A little folding of the hands to rest;
So shall your poverty come like a prowler,
And your need like an armed man.

Proverbs 24:30–34

The lazy man will not plow because of winter;
He will beg during harvest and have nothing.

Proverbs 20:4

Better is a little with righteousness,
Than vast revenues without justice.

Proverbs 16:8

For *"the earth is the LORD's, and all its fullness."*
I Corinthians 10:26

So that you do not appear to men to be fasting, but to your Father who is in the secret place; and your Father who sees in secret will reward you openly.

Do not lay up for yourselves treasures on earth, where moth and rust destroy and where thieves break in and steal;

But lay up for yourselves treasures in heaven, where neither moth nor rust destroys and where thieves do not break in and steal.

For where your treasure is, there your heart will be also.

Matthew 6:18–21

Then you will prosper, if you take care to fulfill the statutes and judgments with which the LORD charged Moses concerning Israel. Be strong and of good courage; do not fear nor be dismayed.

I Chronicles 22:13

For the love of money is a root of all kinds of evil, for which some have strayed from the faith in their greediness, and pierced themselves through with many sorrows.

I Timothy 6:10

The LORD makes poor and makes rich;
He brings low and lifts up.
He raises the poor from the dust
And lifts the beggar from the ash heap,
To set them among princes
And make them inherit the throne of glory.

For the pillars of the earth are the LORD's,
And He has set the world upon them.
He will guard the feet of His saints,
But the wicked shall be silent in darkness.
For by strength no man shall prevail.

I Samuel 2:7–9

Bring your tithe into
the storehouse

∞

Honor the LORD with your possessions,
And with the firstfruits of all your increase;
So your barns will be filled with plenty,
And your vats will overflow with new wine.

Proverbs 3:9–10

The righteous shall flourish like a palm tree,
He shall grow like a cedar in Lebanon.

Psalm 92:12

Give, and it will be given to you: good measure, pressed down, shaken together, and running over will be put into your bosom. For with the same measure that you use, it will be measured back to you.

Luke 6:38

Three times a year all your males shall appear before the LORD your God in the place which He chooses: at the Feast of Unleavened Bread, at the Feast of Weeks, and at the Feast of Tabernacles; and they shall not appear before the LORD empty-handed.

Every man shall give as he is able, according to the blessing of the LORD your God which He has given you.

Deuteronomy 16:16–17

"Will a man rob God?
Yet you have robbed Me!
But you say,
'In what way have we robbed You?'
In tithes and offerings.
You are cursed with a curse,
For you have robbed Me,
Even this whole nation.
Bring all the tithes into the storehouse,
That there may be food in My house,
And try Me now in this,"
Says the LORD of hosts,
"If I will not open for you the windows of heaven
And pour out for you such blessing
That there will not be room enough to receive it.
And I will rebuke the devourer for your sakes,
So that he will not destroy the fruit of your ground,
Nor shall the vine fail to bear fruit for you in the field,"
Says the LORD of hosts;
"And all nations will call you blessed,

For you will be a delightful land,"
Says the LORD of hosts.

Malachi 3:8–12

Now concerning the collection for the saints, as I have given orders to the churches of Galatia, so you must do also:

On the first day of the week let each one of you lay something aside, storing up as he may prosper, that there be no collections when I come.

I Corinthians 16:1–2

Give to the LORD, O families of the peoples,
Give to the LORD glory and strength.
Give to the LORD the glory due His name;
Bring an offering, and come into His courts.
Oh, worship the LORD in the beauty of holiness!
Tremble before Him, all the earth.

Psalm 96:7–9

But this I say: He who sows sparingly will also reap sparingly, and he who sows bountifully will also reap bountifully.

So let each one give as he purposes in his heart, not grudgingly or of necessity; for God loves a cheerful giver.

And God is able to make all grace abound toward

you, that you, always having all sufficiency in all things, may have an abundance for every good work.

As it is written: *"He has dispersed abroad,*
He has given to the poor; His righteousness endures
forever."

Now may He who supplies seed to the sower, and bread for food, supply and multiply the seed you have sown and increase the fruits of your righteousness,

while you are enriched in everything for all liberality, which causes thanksgiving through us to God.

For the administration of this service not only supplies the needs of the saints, but also is abounding through many thanksgivings to God.

II Corinthians 9:6–12

GOD LISTENS TO YOUR PRAYERS WHEN

Your children disappoint you

∞

A wise servant will rule over a son who causes
shame,
And will share an inheritance among the brothers.

Proverbs 17:2

For if the firstfruit is holy, the lump is also holy; and
if the root is holy, so are the branches.

Romans 11:16

(For the LORD your God is a merciful God), He
will not forsake you nor destroy you, nor forget the
covenant of your fathers which He swore to them.

Deuteronomy 4:31

Those who are planted in the house of the LORD
Shall flourish in the courts of our God.
They shall still bear fruit in old age;
They shall be fresh and flourishing,
To declare that the LORD is upright;
He is my rock, and there is no unrighteousness
in Him.

Psalm 92:13–15

Then I said, "I have labored in vain,
I have spent my strength for nothing and in vain;
Yet surely my just reward is with the LORD,
And my work with my God."
Thus says the LORD:
"In an acceptable time I have heard You,
And in the day of salvation I have helped You;
I will preserve You and give You
As a covenant to the people,
To restore the earth,
To cause them to inherit the desolate heritages;
That You may say to the prisoners, 'Go forth,'
To those who are in darkness, 'Show yourselves.'
They shall feed along the roads,
And their pastures shall be on all desolate heights.
They shall neither hunger nor thirst,
Neither heat nor sun shall strike them;
For He who has mercy on them will lead them,
Even by the springs of water He will guide them.
I will make each of My mountains a road, and My
highways shall be elevated."

Isaiah 49:4, 8–11

For I know of nothing against myself, yet I am
not justified by this; but He who judges me is the
Lord.

Therefore judge nothing before the time, until the

Lord comes, who will both bring to light the hidden things of darkness and reveal the counsels of the hearts. Then each one's praise will come from God.

1 Corinthians 4:4–5

Who would form a god or mold an image
That profits him nothing?

Isaiah 44:10

He heals the brokenhearted
And binds up their wounds.

Psalm 147:3

Now the sons of Eli were corrupt; they did not know the LORD.

And the priests' custom with the people was that when any man offered a sacrifice, the priest's servant would come with a three-pronged fleshhook in his hand while the meat was boiling.

Also, before they burned the fat, the priest's servant would come and say to the man who sacrificed, "Give meat for roasting to the priest, for he will not take boiled meat from you, but raw."

And if the man said to him, "They should really burn the fat first; then you may take as much as your heart desires," he would then answer him, "No, but you must give it now; and if not, I will take it by force."

Therefore the sin of the young men was very great before the LORD, for men abhorred the offering of the LORD.

Now Eli was very old; and he heard everything his sons did to all Israel, and how they lay with the women who assembled at the door of the tabernacle of meeting.

So he said to them, "Why do you do such things? For I hear of your evil dealings from all the people.

"No, my sons! For it is not a good report that I hear. You make the LORD's people transgress.

"If one man sins against another, God will judge him. But if a man sins against the LORD, who will intercede for him?" Nevertheless they did not heed the voice of their father, because the LORD desired to kill them.

I Samuel 2:12–13, 15–17, 22–25

Just then the Cushite came, and the Cushite said, "There is good news, my lord the king! For the LORD has avenged you this day of all those who rose against you."

And the king said to the Cushite, "Is the young man Absalom safe?" So the Cushite answered, "May the enemies of my lord the king, and all who rise against you to do harm, be like that young man!"

Then the king was deeply moved, and went up to

the chamber over the gate, and wept. And as he went, he said thus: "O my son Absalom—my son, my son Absalom—if only I had died in your place! O Absalom my son, my son!"

II Samuel 18:31–33

For a mere moment I have forsaken you,
But with great mercies I will gather you.
All your children shall be taught by the LORD,
And great shall be the peace of your children.

Isaiah 54:7, 13

All we like sheep have gone astray;
We have turned, every one, to his own way;
And the LORD has laid on Him the iniquity of us all.

Isaiah 53:6

For the LORD will not cast off His people,
Nor will He forsake His inheritance.
But judgment will return to righteousness,
And all the upright in heart will follow it.

Psalm 94:14–15

So the ransomed of the LORD shall return,
And come to Zion with singing,
With everlasting joy on their heads.

They shall obtain joy and gladness;
Sorrow and sighing shall flee away.

Isaiah 51:11

I will not leave you orphans; I will come to you.

John 14:18

You ask for His patience

∞

Fathers, do not provoke your children, lest they become discouraged.

Colossians 3:21

Blessed is he who waits.

Daniel 12:12a

The end of a thing is better than its beginning;
The patient in spirit is better than the proud in spirit.

Ecclesiastes 7:8

My brethren, count it all joy when you fall into various trials,
knowing that the testing of your faith produces patience.
But let patience have its perfect work, that you may be perfect and complete, lacking nothing.

James 1:2–4

Now we exhort you, brethren, warn those who are unruly, comfort the fainthearted, uphold the weak, be patient with all.

I Thessalonians 5:14

And a servant of the Lord must not quarrel but be gentle to all, able to teach, patient.

II Timothy 2:24

Therefore we also, since we are surrounded by so great a cloud of witnesses, let us lay aside every weight, and the sin which so easily ensnares us, and let us run with endurance the race that is set before us.

Hebrews 12:1

For even Christ did not please Himself; but as it is written, *"The reproaches of those who reproached You fell on Me."*

For whatever things were written before were written for our learning, that we through the patience and comfort of the Scriptures might have hope.

Now may the God of patience and comfort grant you to be like-minded toward one another, according to Christ Jesus.

Romans 15:3–5

And not only that, but we also glory in tribulations, knowing that tribulation produces perseverance.

Romans 5:3

Therefore if there is any consolation in Christ, if any comfort of love, if any fellowship of the Spirit, if any affection and mercy, fulfill my joy by being like-minded, having the same love, being of one accord, of one mind.

Let nothing be done through selfish ambition or conceit, but in lowliness of mind let each esteem others better than himself.

Let each of you look out not only for his own interests, but also for the interests of others.

Philippians 2:1–4

You ask for His Spirit's guidance

∞

What then shall we say to these things? If God is for us, who can be against us?

He who did not spare His own Son, but delivered Him up for us all, how shall He not with Him also freely give us all things?

Romans 8:31–32

Teach me to do Your will,
For You are my God;
Your Spirit is good.
Lead me in the land of uprightness.
Revive me, O LORD, for Your name's sake!
For Your righteousness' sake bring my soul out of trouble.

Psalm 143:10–11

Now the Lord is the Spirit; and where the Spirit of the Lord is, there is liberty.

But we all, with unveiled face, beholding as in a mirror the glory of the Lord, are being transformed into the same image from glory to glory, just as by the Spirit of the Lord.

II Corinthians 3:17–18

For He shall give His angels charge over you,
To keep you in all your ways.
In their hands they shall bear you up,
Lest you dash your foot against a stone.
You shall tread upon the lion and the cobra,
The young lion and the serpent you shall trample
underfoot.
"Because he has set his love upon Me, therefore I
will deliver him;
I will set him on high, because he has known My
name.
He shall call upon Me, and I will answer him;
I will be with him in trouble;
I will deliver him and honor him.
With long life I will satisfy him,
And show him My salvation."

Psalm 91:11–16

By this we know that we abide in Him, and He in us,
because He has given us of His Spirit.

I John 4:13

I say then: Walk in the Spirit, and you shall not fulfill the lust of the flesh.

For the flesh lusts against the Spirit, and the Spirit
against the flesh; and these are contrary to one another,
so that you do not do the things that you wish.

But if you are led by the Spirit, you are not under the law.

Now the works of the flesh are evident, which are: adultery, fornication, uncleanness, lewdness,

idolatry, sorcery, hatred, contentions, jealousies, outbursts of wrath, selfish ambitions, dissensions, heresies,

envy, murders, drunkenness, revelries, and the like; of which I tell you beforehand, just as I also told you in time past, that those who practice such things will not inherit the kingdom of God.

But the fruit of the Spirit is love, joy, peace, long-suffering, kindness, goodness, faithfulness,

gentleness, self-control. Against such there is no law.

And those who are Christ's have crucified the flesh with its passions and desires.

If we live in the Spirit, let us also walk in the Spirit.

Let us not become conceited, provoking one another, envying one another.

Galatians 5:16–26

For we through the Spirit eagerly wait for the hope of righteousness by faith.

Galatians 5:5

But God has revealed them to us through His Spirit. For the Spirit searches all things, yes, the deep things of God.

For what man knows the things of a man except the spirit of the man which is in him? Even so no one knows the things of God except the Spirit of God.

Now we have received, not the spirit of the world, but the Spirit who is from God, that we might know the things that have been freely given to us by God.

These things we also speak, not in words which man's wisdom teaches but which the Holy Spirit teaches, comparing spiritual things with spiritual.

But the natural man does not receive the things of the Spirit of God, for they are foolishness to him; nor can he know them, because they are spiritually discerned.

But he who is spiritual judges all things, yet he himself is rightly judged by no one.

For *"who has known the mind of the LORD that he may instruct Him?"* But we have the mind of Christ.

I Corinthians 2:10–16

You admit your shortcomings as a father

∞

O God, do not be far from me;
O my God, make haste to help me!
My mouth shall tell of Your righteousness
And Your salvation all the day,
For I do not know their limits.
I will go in the strength of the Lord GOD;
I will make mention of Your righteousness, of
Yours only.
O God, You have taught me from my youth;
And to this day I declare Your wondrous works.
Now also when I am old and grayheaded,
O God, do not forsake me,
Until I declare Your strength to this generation,
Your power to everyone who is to come.

Psalm 71:12, 15–18

Be of good courage,
And He shall strengthen your heart,
All you who hope in the LORD.

Psalm 31:24

He who covers his sins will not prosper,
But whoever confesses and forsakes them will have
mercy.

Proverbs 28:13

For I will pour water on him who is thirsty,
And floods on the dry ground;
I will pour My Spirit on your descendants,
And My blessing on your offspring;
They will spring up among the grass
Like willows by the watercourses.

Isaiah 44:3–4

Only take heed to yourself, and diligently keep
yourself, lest you forget the things your eyes have seen,
and lest they depart from your heart all the days of
your life. And teach them to your children and your
grandchildren.

Deuteronomy 4:9

Now it shall come to pass, if you diligently obey the
voice of the LORD your God, to observe carefully all His
commandments which I command you today, that the
LORD your God will set you high above all nations of
the earth.

Blessed shall be the fruit of your body, the produce of

your ground and the increase of your herds, the increase of your cattle and the offspring of your flocks.

Deuteronomy 28:1, 4

So then neither he who plants is anything, nor he who waters, but God who gives the increase.

Now he who plants and he who waters are one, and each one will receive his own reward according to his own labor.

For we are God's fellow workers; you are God's field, you are God's building.

I Corinthians 3:7–9

The LORD is good,
A stronghold in the day of trouble;
And He knows those who trust in Him.

Nahum 1:7

"For how can this servant of my lord talk with you, my lord? As for me, no strength remains in me now, nor is any breath left in me."

Then again, the one having the likeness of a man touched me and strengthened me.

And he said, "O man greatly beloved, fear not! Peace be to you; be strong, yes, be strong!" So when he spoke to me I was strengthened, and said, "Let my lord speak, for you have strengthened me."

Then he said, "Do you know why I have come to

you? And now I must return to fight with the prince of Persia; and when I have gone forth, indeed the prince of Greece will come.

"But I will tell you what is noted in the Scripture of Truth. (No one upholds me against these, except Michael your prince.)"

Daniel 10:17–21

Call to Me, and I will answer you, and show you great and mighty things, which you do not know.

Jeremiah 33:3

The LORD is far from the wicked,
But He hears the prayer of the righteous.
The light of the eyes rejoices the heart,
And a good report makes the bones healthy.
The ear that hears the rebukes of life
Will abide among the wise.
He who disdains instruction despises his own soul,
But he who heeds rebuke gets understanding.
The fear of the LORD is the instruction of wisdom,
And before honor is humility.

Proverbs 15:29–33

You're overwhelmed by your family responsibilities
∞

Unless the LORD builds the house,
They labor in vain who build it;
Unless the LORD guards the city,
The watchman stays awake in vain.
It is vain for you to rise up early,
To sit up late,
To eat the bread of sorrows;
For so He gives His beloved sleep.
Behold, children are a heritage from the LORD,
The fruit of the womb is a reward.
Like arrows in the hand of a warrior,
So are the children of one's youth.
Happy is the man who has his quiver full of them;
They shall not be ashamed,
But shall speak with their enemies in the gate.

Psalm 127:1–5

"For the mountains shall depart
And the hills be removed,
But My kindness shall not depart from you,

Nor shall My covenant of peace be removed,"
Says the LORD, who has mercy on you.

Isaiah 54:10

I cried out to God with my voice—
To God with my voice;
And He gave ear to me.
I remembered God, and was troubled;
I complained, and my spirit was overwhelmed. Selah.

Psalm 77:1, 3

Trust in the LORD with all your heart,
And lean not on your own understanding;
In all your ways acknowledge Him,
And He shall direct your paths.
Do not be wise in your own eyes;
Fear the LORD and depart from evil.

Proverbs 3:5–7

Lift up your eyes on high,
And see who has created these things,
Who brings out their host by number;
He calls them all by name,
By the greatness of His might
And the strength of His power;
Not one is missing.

Isaiah 40:26

He gives power to the weak,
And to those who have no might
He increases strength.

Isaiah 40:29

When you pass through the waters, I will be with
you;
And through the rivers, they shall not overflow you.
When you walk through the fire, you shall not be
burned,
Nor shall the flame scorch you.

Isaiah 43:2

"Fear not, for I am with you;
I will bring your descendants from the east,
And gather you from the west;
I will say to the north, 'Give them up!'
And to the south, 'Do not keep them back!'
Bring My sons from afar,
And My daughters from the ends of the earth—
Everyone who is called by My name,
Whom I have created for My glory;
I have formed him, yes, I have made him."

Isaiah 43:5–7

Be strong and of good courage, do not fear nor be
afraid of them; for the LORD your God, He is the One

who goes with you. He will not leave you nor forsake you.

Deuteronomy 31:6

Therefore, brethren, stand fast and hold the traditions which you were taught, whether by word or our epistle.

Now may our Lord Jesus Christ Himself, and our God and Father, who has loved us and given us everlasting consolation and good hope by grace,

comfort your hearts and establish you in every good word and work.

II Thessalonians 2:15–17

GOD FILLS YOU WITH JOY WHEN

Your family gives praises to the Lord

∞

I will extol You, my God, O King;
And I will bless Your name forever and ever.
Every day I will bless You,
And I will praise Your name forever and ever.
Great is the LORD, and greatly to be praised;
And His greatness is unsearchable.
One generation shall praise Your works to another,
And shall declare Your mighty acts.

Psalm 145:1–4

Both young men and maidens;
Old men and children.
Let them praise the name of the LORD,
For His name alone is exalted;
His glory is above the earth and heaven.
And He has exalted the horn of His people,
The praise of all His saints—
Of the children of Israel,
A people near to Him.
Praise the LORD!

Psalm 148:12–14

Praise the LORD!
Praise God in His sanctuary;
Praise Him in His mighty firmament!
Praise Him for His mighty acts;
Praise Him according to His excellent greatness!
Praise Him with the sound of the trumpet;
Praise Him with the lute and harp!
Praise Him with the timbrel and dance;
Praise Him with stringed instruments and flutes!
Praise Him with loud cymbals;
Praise Him with clashing cymbals!
Let everything that has breath praise the LORD.
Praise the LORD!

Psalm 150:1–6

This people I have formed for Myself;
They shall declare My praise.

Isaiah 43:21

I will call upon the LORD, who is worthy to be
praised;
So shall I be saved from my enemies.

II Samuel 22:4

Know that the LORD, He is God;
It is He who has made us, and not we ourselves;
We are His people and the sheep of His pasture.
Enter into His gates with thanksgiving,

And into His courts with praise.
Be thankful to Him, and bless His name.
For the LORD is good;
His mercy is everlasting,
And His truth endures to all generations.

Psalm 100:3–5

I will sing of the mercies of the LORD forever;
With my mouth will I make known Your
faithfulness to all generations.
For I have said, "Mercy shall be built up forever;
Your faithfulness You shall establish in the very
heavens.
I have made a covenant with My chosen,
I have sworn to My servant David:
'Your seed I will establish forever,
And build up your throne to all generations.' Selah.

Psalm 89:1–4

This will be written for the generation to come,
That a people yet to be created may praise the LORD.

Psalm 102:18

"Sing and rejoice, O daughter of Zion! For behold,
I am coming and I will dwell in your midst," says the
LORD.

Zechariah 2:10

Nebuchadnezzar the king,
To all peoples, nations, and languages that dwell in
all the earth:
Peace be multiplied to you.
I thought it good to declare the signs and wonders
that the Most High God has worked for me.
How great are His signs,
And how mighty His wonders!
His kingdom is an everlasting kingdom,
And His dominion is from generation to generation.

Daniel 4:1–3

I thank You and praise You,
O God of my fathers;
You have given me wisdom and might,
And have now made known to me what we asked
of You,
For You have made known to us the king's demand.

Daniel 2:23

But you are a chosen generation, a royal priesthood,
a holy nation, His own special people, that you may proclaim the praises of Him who called you out of darkness
into His marvelous light.

I Peter 2:9

May the LORD give you increase more and more,
You and your children.

May you be blessed by the LORD,
Who made heaven and earth.
The heaven, even the heavens, are the LORD's;
But the earth He has given to the children of men.
The dead do not praise the LORD,
Nor any who go down into silence.
But we will bless the LORD
From this time forth and forevermore.
Praise the LORD!

Psalm 115:14–18

Your children grow to love Him

∞

I love those who love me,
And those who seek me diligently will find me.

Proverbs 8:17

And the child Samuel grew in stature, and in favor both with the LORD and men.

I Samuel 2:26

The LORD will establish you as a holy people to Himself, just as He has sworn to you, if you keep the commandments of the LORD your God and walk in His ways.

Then all peoples of the earth shall see that you are called by the name of the LORD, and they shall be afraid of you.

Deuteronomy 28:9–10

You are the salt of the earth; but if the salt loses its flavor, how shall it be seasoned? It is then good for nothing but to be thrown out and trampled underfoot by men.

You are the light of the world. A city that is set on a hill cannot be hidden.

Nor do they light a lamp and put it under a basket, but on a lampstand, and it gives light to all who are in the house.

Let your light so shine before men, that they may see your good works and glorify your Father in heaven.

Matthew 5:13–16

That Christ may dwell in your hearts through faith; that you, being rooted and grounded in love,

may be able to comprehend with all the saints what is the width and length and depth and height—

to know the love of Christ which passes knowledge; that you may be filled with all the fullness of God.

Ephesians 3:17–19

"At the same time," says the LORD, "I will be the God of all the families of Israel, and they shall be My people."

The LORD has appeared of old to me, saying:

"Yes, I have loved you with an everlasting love;

Therefore with lovingkindness I have drawn you."

Jeremiah 31:1, 3

Knowledge puffs up, but love edifies.

And if anyone thinks that he knows anything, he knows nothing yet as he ought to know.

But if anyone loves God, this one is known by Him.

I Corinthians 8:1b–3

"And you shall love the LORD your God with all your heart, with all your soul, with all your mind, and with all your strength." This is the first commandment.

Mark 12:30

Grace to you and peace from God our Father and the Lord Jesus Christ.

I thank my God always concerning you for the grace of God which was given to you by Christ Jesus,

that you were enriched in everything by Him in all utterance and all knowledge,

even as the testimony of Christ was confirmed in you,

so that you come short in no gift, eagerly waiting for the revelation of our Lord Jesus Christ,

who will also confirm you to the end, that you may be blameless in the day of our Lord Jesus Christ.

God is faithful, by whom you were called into the fellowship of His Son, Jesus Christ our Lord.

I Corinthians 1:3–9

Your family worships together

∞

Then we cried out to the LORD God of our fathers, and the LORD heard our voice and looked on our affliction and our labor and our oppression.

Deuteronomy 26:7

"And now, behold, I have brought the firstfruits of the land which you, O LORD, have given me."
Then you shall set it before the LORD your God, and worship before the LORD your God.

Deuteronomy 26:10

Oh come, let us worship and bow down;
Let us kneel before the LORD our Maker.
For He is our God,
And we are the people of His pasture,
And the sheep of His hand.

Psalm 95:6, 7

Also with the lute I will praise You—
And Your faithfulness, O my God!
To You I will sing with the harp,
O Holy One of Israel.

My lips shall greatly rejoice when I sing to You,
And my soul, which You have redeemed.
My tongue also shall talk of Your righteousness all the
day long;
For they are confounded,
For they are brought to shame
Who seek my hurt.

Psalm 71:22–24

The LORD lives!
Blessed be my Rock!
Let God be exalted,
The Rock of my salvation!

II Samuel 22:47

Exalt the LORD our God,
And worship at His holy hill;
For the LORD our God is holy.
Make a joyful shout to the LORD, all you lands!
Serve the LORD with gladness;
Come before His presence with singing.

Psalm 99:9; 100:1–2

Let them give glory to the LORD,
And declare His praise in the coastlands.

Isaiah 42:12

To whom then will you liken God?
Or what likeness will you compare to Him?
Have you not known?
Have you not heard?
Has it not been told you from the beginning?
Have you not understood from the foundations
of the earth?
It is He who sits above the circle of the earth,
And its inhabitants are like grasshoppers,
Who stretches out the heavens like a curtain,
And spreads them out like a tent to dwell in.

Isaiah 40:18, 21–22

This people I have formed for Myself;
They shall declare My praise.

Isaiah 43:21

Therefore My people shall know My name;
Therefore they shall know in that day
That I am He who speaks:
"Behold, it is I."

Isaiah 52:6

Then you shall delight yourself in the LORD;
And I will cause you to ride on the high hills of
the earth,

And feed you with the heritage of Jacob your father.
The mouth of the LORD has spoken.

Isaiah 58:14

Jesus said to her, "Woman, believe Me, the hour is coming when you will neither on this mountain, nor in Jerusalem, worship the Father.

"You worship what you do not know; we know what we worship, for salvation is of the Jews.

"But the hour is coming, and now is, when the true worshipers will worship the Father in spirit and truth; for the Father is seeking such to worship Him.

"God is Spirit, and those who worship Him must worship in spirit and truth."

John 4:21–24

Then Jesus said to him, "Away with you, Satan! For it is written, *'You shall worship the LORD your God, and Him only you shall serve.'*"

Matthew 4:10

Then Paul stood in the midst of the Areopagus and said, "Men of Athens, I perceive that in all things you are very religious;

"for as I was passing through and considering the objects of your worship, I even found an altar with this inscription: TO THE UNKNOWN GOD. Therefore, the One whom you worship without knowing, Him I proclaim to you.

"For in Him we live and move and have our being, as also some of your own poets have said, 'For we are also His offspring.'

"Therefore, since we are the offspring of God, we ought not to think that the Divine Nature is like gold or silver or stone, something shaped by art and man's devising.

"Truly, these times of ignorance God overlooked, but now commands all men everywhere to repent."

Acts 17:22–23, 28–30

Let the word of Christ dwell in you richly in all wisdom, teaching and admonishing one another in psalms and hymns and spiritual songs, singing with grace in your hearts to the Lord.

Colossians 3:16

GOD KEEPS
YOU SECURE WHEN

Your family faces its enemies

∞

The eternal God is your refuge,
And underneath are the everlasting arms;
He will thrust out the enemy from before you,
And will say, "Destroy!"

Deuteronomy 33:27

Be strong and of good courage, do not fear nor be afraid of them; for the LORD your God, He is the One who goes with you. He will not leave you nor forsake you.

Deuteronomy 31:6

But if you indeed obey His voice and do all that I speak, then I will be an enemy to your enemies and an adversary to your adversaries.

Exodus 23:22

Arise, O LORD!
O God, lift up Your hand!
Do not forget the humble.
Why do the wicked renounce God?
He has said in his heart,
"You will not require an account."
But You have seen, for You observe trouble and grief,

To repay it by Your hand.
The helpless commits himself to You;
You are the helper of the fatherless.
Break the arm of the wicked and the evil man;
Seek out his wickedness until You find none.
The LORD is King forever and ever;
The nations have perished out of His land.
LORD, You have heard the desire of the humble;
You will prepare their heart;
You will cause Your ear to hear,
To do justice to the fatherless and the oppressed,
That the man of the earth may oppress no more.

Psalm 10:12–18

He permitted no one to do them wrong;
Yes, He rebuked kings for their sakes,
Saying, "Do not touch My anointed ones,
And do My prophets no harm."

Psalm 105:14–15

Then the king arose very early in the morning and went in haste to the den of lions.

And when he came to the den, he cried out with a lamenting voice to Daniel. The king spoke, saying to Daniel, "Daniel, servant of the living God, has your God, whom you serve continually, been able to deliver you from the lions?"

Then Daniel said to the king, "O king, live forever!

"My God sent His angel and shut the lions' mouths, so that they have not hurt me, because I was found innocent before Him; and also, O king, I have done no wrong before you."

Daniel 6:19–22

Do not keep silent, O God!
Do not hold Your peace,
And do not be still, O God!
For behold, Your enemies make a tumult;
And those who hate You have lifted up their head.
They have taken crafty counsel against Your people,
And consulted together against Your sheltered ones.

Psalm 83:1–3

Shadrach, Meshach, and Abed-Nego answered and said to the king, "O Nebuchadnezzar, we have no need to answer you in this matter.

"If that is the case, our God whom we serve is able to deliver us from the burning fiery furnace, and He will deliver us from your hand, O king.

"But if not, let it be known to you, O king, that we do not serve your gods, nor will we worship the gold image which you have set up."

Then Nebuchadnezzar was full of fury, and the expression on his face changed toward Shadrach, Meshach, and Abed-Nego. He spoke and commanded that they heat the furnace seven times more than it was usually heated.

And these three men, Shadrach, Meshach, and Abed-Nego, fell down bound into the midst of the burning fiery furnace.

Then King Nebuchadnezzar was astonished; and he rose in haste and spoke, saying to his counselors, "Did we not cast three men bound into the midst of the fire?" They answered and said to the king, "True, O king."

"Look!" he answered, "I see four men loose, walking in the midst of the fire; and they are not hurt, and the form of the fourth is like the Son of God."

Daniel 3:16–19, 23–25

Therefore submit to God. Resist the devil and he will flee from you.

James 4:7

I will love You, O LORD, my strength.
The LORD is my rock and my fortress and my deliverer;
My God, my strength, in whom I will trust;
My shield and the horn of my salvation, my stronghold.
I will call upon the LORD, who is worthy to be praised;
So shall I be saved from my enemies.

Psalm 18:1–3

You need to make
a major job change

∞

Do not overwork to be rich;
Because of your own understanding, cease!
Will you set your eyes on that which is not?
For riches certainly make themselves wings;
They fly away like an eagle toward heaven.

Proverbs 23:4–5

Do not put your trust in princes,
Nor in a son of man, in whom there is no help.
His spirit departs, he returns to his earth;
In that very day his plans perish.
Happy is he who has the God of Jacob for his help,
Whose hope is in the LORD his God.

Psalm 146:3–5

Again, I saw that for all toil and every skillful work
a man is envied by his neighbor. This also is vanity and
grasping for the wind.
The fool folds his hands
And consumes his own flesh.
Better a handful with quietness

Than both hands full, together with toil and grasping for the wind.

Ecclesiastes 4:4–6

For the Scripture says, "You shall not muzzle an ox while it treads out the grain," and, "The laborer is worthy of his wages."

I Timothy 5:18

What profit has the worker from that in which he labors?

I have seen the God-given task with which the sons of men are to be occupied.

He has made everything beautiful in its time. Also He has put eternity in their hearts, except that no one can find out the work that God does from beginning to end.

I know that nothing is better for them than to rejoice, and to do good in their lives,

and also that every man should eat and drink and enjoy the good of all his labor—it is the gift of God.

Ecclesiastes 3:9–13

Then I hated all my labor in which I had toiled under the sun, because I must leave it to the man who will come after me.

And who knows whether he will be wise or a fool?

Yet he will rule over all my labor in which I toiled and in which I have shown myself wise under the sun. This also is vanity.

Therefore I turned my heart and despaired of all the labor in which I had toiled under the sun.

For God gives wisdom and knowledge and joy to a man who is good in His sight; but to the sinner He gives the work of gathering and collecting, that he may give to him who is good before God. This also is vanity and grasping for the wind.

Ecclesiastes 2:18–20, 26

The name of the LORD is a strong tower;
The righteous run to it and are safe.
Proverbs 18:10

Therefore I say to you, do not worry about your life, what you will eat or what you will drink; nor about your body, what you will put on. Is not life more than food and the body more than clothing?

Look at the birds of the air, for they neither sow nor reap nor gather into barns; yet your heavenly Father feeds them. Are you not of more value than they?

Which of you by worrying can add one cubit to his stature?

So why do you worry about clothing? Consider the

lilies of the field, how they grow: they neither toil nor spin;

and yet I say to you that even Solomon in all his glory was not arrayed like one of these.

Now if God so clothes the grass of the field, which today is, and tomorrow is thrown into the oven, will He not much more clothe you, O you of little faith?

Therefore do not worry, saying, "What shall we eat?" or "What shall we drink?" or "What shall we wear?"

For after all these things the Gentiles seek. For your heavenly Father knows that you need all these things.

But seek first the kingdom of God and His righteousness, and all these things shall be added to you.

Therefore do not worry about tomorrow, for tomorrow will worry about its own things. Sufficient for the day is its own trouble.

Matthew 6:25–34

For no other foundation can anyone lay than that which is laid, which is Jesus Christ.

Now if anyone builds on this foundation with gold, silver, precious stones, wood, hay, straw,

each one's work will become clear; for the Day will declare it, because it will be revealed by fire; and the fire will test each one's work, of what sort it is.

If anyone's work which he has built on it endures, he will receive a reward.

If anyone's work is burned, he will suffer loss; but he himself will be saved, yet so as through fire.

I Corinthians 3:11–15

You worry about your family's health and well-being

∞

For I will pour water on him who is thirsty,
And floods on the dry ground;
I will pour My Spirit on your descendants,
And My blessing on your offspring.

Isaiah 44:3

The father of the righteous will greatly rejoice,
And he who begets a wise child will delight in
him.
Let your father and your mother be glad,
And let her who bore you rejoice.
My son, give me your heart,
And let your eyes observe my ways.

Proverbs 23:24–26

You will keep him in perfect peace,
Whose mind is stayed on You,
Because he trusts in You.

Isaiah 26:3

The eyes of all look expectantly to You,
And You give them their food in due season.

You open Your hand
And satisfy the desire of every living thing.
The LORD is righteous in all His ways,
Gracious in all His works.
The LORD is near to all who call upon Him,
To all who call upon Him in truth.
He will fulfill the desire of those who fear Him;
He also will hear their cry and save them.
The LORD preserves all who love Him,
But all the wicked He will destroy.
My mouth shall speak the praise of the LORD,
And all flesh shall bless His holy name
Forever and ever.

Psalm 145:15–21

The work of righteousness will be peace,
And the effect of righteousness, quietness and
assurance forever.

Isaiah 32:17

Now behold, Boaz came from Bethlehem, and said
to the reapers, "The LORD be with you!" And they
answered him, "The LORD bless you!"

Then Boaz said to his servant who was in charge of
the reapers, "Whose young woman is this?"

So the servant who was in charge of the reapers
answered and said, "It is the young Moabite woman who
came back with Naomi from the country of Moab.

"And she said, 'Please let me glean and gather after the reapers among the sheaves.' So she came and has continued from morning until now, though she rested a little in the house."

Then Boaz said to Ruth, "You will listen, my daughter, will you not? Do not go to glean in another field, nor go from here, but stay close by my young women.

"Let your eyes be on the field which they reap, and go after them. Have I not commanded the young men not to touch you? And when you are thirsty, go to the vessels and drink from what the young men have drawn."

So she fell on her face, bowed down to the ground, and said to him, "Why have I found favor in your eyes, that you should take notice of me, since I am a foreigner?"

And Boaz answered and said to her, "It has been fully reported to me, all that you have done for your mother-in-law since the death of your husband, and how you have left your father and your mother and the land of your birth, and have come to a people whom you did not know before.

"The LORD repay your work, and a full reward be given you by the LORD God of Israel, under whose wings you have come for refuge."

Ruth 2:4–12

Blessed is every one who fears the LORD,
Who walks in His ways.

When you eat the labor of your hands,
You shall be happy, and it shall be well with you.
Your wife shall be like a fruitful vine
In the very heart of your house,
Your children like olive plants
All around your table.
Behold, thus shall the man be blessed
Who fears the LORD.
The LORD bless you out of Zion,
And may you see the good of Jerusalem all the
days of your life.
Yes, may you see your children's children.
Peace be upon Israel!

Psalm 128:1–6

But because the LORD loves you, and because He would keep the oath which He swore to your fathers, the LORD has brought you out with a mighty hand, and redeemed you from the house of bondage, from the hand of Pharaoh king of Egypt.

Therefore know that the LORD your God, He is God, the faithful God who keeps covenant and mercy for a thousand generations with those who love Him and keep His commandments.

Deuteronomy 7:8–9

I will both lie down in peace, and sleep;
For You alone, O LORD, make me dwell in safety.

Psalm 4:8

Your mercy, O LORD, is in the heavens;
Your faithfulness reaches to the clouds.

Psalm 36:5

Blessed be the Lord,
Who daily loads us with benefits,
The God of our salvation! Selah.

Psalm 68:19

Your child has trouble succeeding in school

∞

Now I say that the heir, as long as he is a child, does not differ at all from a slave, though he is master of all,

but is under guardians and stewards until the time appointed by the father.

Galatians 4:1–2

Let no one deceive himself. If anyone among you seems to be wise in this age, let him become a fool that he may become wise.

For the wisdom of this world is foolishness with God. For it is written, *"He catches the wise in their own craftiness."*

I Corinthians 3:18–19

For you see your calling, brethren, that not many wise according to the flesh, not many mighty, not many noble, are called.

But God has chosen the foolish things of the world to put to shame the wise, and God has chosen the weak things of the world to put to shame the things which are mighty;

and the base things of the world and the things which are despised God has chosen, and the things which are not, to bring to nothing the things that are,

that no flesh should glory in His presence.

I Corinthians 1:26–29

And further, my son, be admonished by these. Of making many books there is no end, and much study is wearisome to the flesh.

Ecclesiastes 12:12

For if anyone thinks himself to be something, when he is nothing, he deceives himself.

But let each one examine his own work, and then he will have rejoicing in himself alone, and not in another.

For each one shall bear his own load.

Let him who is taught the word share in all good things with him who teaches.

Do not be deceived, God is not mocked; for whatever a man sows, that he will also reap.

Galatians 6:3–7

Then the king instructed Ashpenaz, the master of his eunuchs, to bring some of the children of Israel and some of the king's descendants and some of the nobles,

young men in whom there was no blemish, but

good-looking, gifted in all wisdom, possessing knowledge and quick to understand, who had ability to serve in the king's palace, and whom they might teach the language and literature of the Chaldeans.

And the king appointed for them a daily provision of the king's delicacies and of the wine which he drank, and three years of training for them, so that at the end of that time they might serve before the king.

Now from among those of the sons of Judah were Daniel, Hananiah, Mishael, and Azariah.

As for these four young men, God gave them knowledge and skill in all literature and wisdom.

Daniel 1:3–6, 17a

Then the secret was revealed to Daniel in a night vision. So Daniel blessed the God of heaven.

Daniel answered and said:

"Blessed be the name of God forever and ever,
For wisdom and might are His.
And He changes the times and the seasons;
He removes kings and raises up kings;
He gives wisdom to the wise
And knowledge to those who have understanding.
He reveals deep and secret things;
He knows what is in the darkness,
And light dwells with Him.
I thank You and praise You,

O God of my fathers;
You have given me wisdom and might,
And have now made known to me what we
asked of You,
For You have made known to us the king's demand."

Daniel 2:19–23

For as we have many members in one body, but all
the members do not have the same function,

so we, being many, are one body in Christ, and
individually members of one another.

Having then gifts differing according to the grace
that is given to us.

Romans 12:4–6a

Do you not know that those who run in a race all
run, but one receives the prize? Run in such a way that
you may obtain it.

And everyone who competes for the prize is temperate in all things. Now they do it to obtain a perishable crown, but we for an imperishable crown.

Therefore I run thus: not with uncertainty. Thus I
fight: not as one who beats the air.

But I discipline my body and bring it into subjection,
lest, when I have preached to others, I myself should
become disqualified.

I Corinthians 9:24–27

You don't have the money to pay the bills

∞

I have been young, and now am old;
Yet I have not seen the righteous forsaken,
Nor his descendants begging bread.
He is ever merciful, and lends;
And his descendants are blessed.
Depart from evil, and do good;
And dwell forevermore.
For the LORD loves justice,
And does not forsake His saints;
They are preserved forever,
But the descendants of the wicked shall be cut off.

Psalm 37:25–28

The young lions lack and suffer hunger;
But those who seek the LORD shall not lack any good thing.

Psalm 34:10

The humble shall see this and be glad;
And you who seek God, your hearts shall live.
For the LORD hears the poor,

And does not despise His prisoners.
Let heaven and earth praise Him,
The seas and everything that moves in them.

Psalm 69:32–34

The LORD will command the blessing on you in
your storehouses and in all to which you set your hand,
and He will bless you in the land which the LORD your
God is giving you.

Deuteronomy 28:8

Wealth and riches will be in his house,
And his righteousness endures forever.

Psalm 112:3

The LORD is my shepherd;
I shall not want.

Psalm 23:1

Ho! Everyone who thirsts,
Come to the waters;
And you who have no money,
Come, buy and eat.
Yes, come, buy wine and milk
Without money and without price.
Why do you spend money for what is not bread,
And your wages for what does not satisfy?
Listen carefully to Me, and eat what is good,

And let your soul delight itself in abundance.
Incline your ear, and come to Me.
Hear, and your soul shall live;
And I will make an everlasting covenant with you—
The sure mercies of David.

Isaiah 55:1–3

The poor and needy seek water, but there is none,
Their tongues fail for thirst.
I, the LORD, will hear them;
I, the God of Israel, will not forsake them.

Isaiah 41:17

I will satiate the soul of the priests with abundance,
And My people shall be satisfied with My
goodness, says the LORD.

Jeremiah 31:14

You shall eat in plenty and be satisfied,
And praise the name of the LORD your God,
Who has dealt wondrously with you;
And My people shall never be put to shame.

Joel 2:26

And my God shall supply all your need according to
His riches in glory by Christ Jesus.

Philippians 4:19

GOD COMFORTS
YOU WHEN

You feel inadequate in rearing your children

∞

For the Lord GOD will help Me;
Therefore I will not be disgraced;
Therefore I have set My face like a flint,
And I know that I will not be ashamed.

Isaiah 50:7

But You are the same,
And Your years will have no end.
The children of Your servants will continue,
And their descendants will be established before You.

Psalm 102:27–28

For the eyes of the LORD run to and fro throughout the whole earth, to show Himself strong on behalf of those whose heart is loyal to Him.

II Chronicles 16:9a

LORD, my heart is not haughty,
Nor my eyes lofty.
Neither do I concern myself with great matters,
Nor with things too profound for me.

Surely I have calmed and quieted my soul,
Like a weaned child with his mother;
Like a weaned child is my soul within me.
O Israel, hope in the LORD
From this time forth and forever.

Psalm 131:1–3

For who makes you differ from another? And what do you have that you did not receive? Now if you did indeed receive it, why do you boast as if you had not received it?

I Corinthians 4:7

But by the grace of God I am what I am, and His grace toward me was not in vain; but I labored more abundantly than they all, yet not I, but the grace of God which was with me.

I Corinthians 15:10

Not that we are sufficient of ourselves to think of anything as being from ourselves, but our sufficiency is from God.

II Corinthians 3:5

Do you know the time when the wild mountain goats bear young?
Or can you mark when the deer gives birth?
Can you number the months that they fulfill?

Or do you know the time when they bear young?
They bow down,
They bring forth their young,
They deliver their offspring.

Job 39:1–3

The wings of the ostrich wave proudly,
But are her wings and pinions like the kindly stork's?
For she leaves her eggs on the ground,
And warms them in the dust;
She forgets that a foot may crush them,
Or that a wild beast may break them.
She treats her young harshly, as though they were not hers;
Her labor is in vain, without concern,
Because God deprived her of wisdom,
And did not endow her with understanding.

Job 39:13–17

By which have been given to us exceedingly great and precious promises, that through these you may be partakers of the divine nature, having escaped the corruption that is in the world through lust.

But also for this very reason, giving all diligence, add to your faith virtue, to virtue knowledge,

to knowledge self-control, to self-control perseverance, to perseverance godliness, to godliness brotherly kindness, and to brotherly kindness love.

For if these things are yours and abound, you will be neither barren nor unfruitful in the knowledge of our Lord Jesus Christ.

II Peter 1:4–8

I have blotted out, like a thick cloud, your transgressions,
And like a cloud, your sins.
Return to Me, for I have redeemed you.

Isaiah 44:22

But we were gentle among you, just as a nursing mother cherishes her own children.

So, affectionately longing for you, we were well pleased to impart to you not only the gospel of God, but also our own lives, because you had become dear to us.

I Thessalonians 2:7–8

I can do all things through Christ who strengthens me.

Philippians 4:13

Come to Me, all you who labor and are heavy laden, and I will give you rest.

Take My yoke upon you and learn from Me, for I

am gentle and lowly in heart, and you will find rest for your souls.

For My yoke is easy and My burden is light.

Matthew 11:28–30

Your child is seriously ill

∞

Beloved, I pray that you may prosper in all things and be in health, just as your soul prospers.

III John 2

Then one of the crowd answered and said, "Teacher, I brought You my son, who has a mute spirit.

"And wherever it seizes him, it throws him down; he foams at the mouth, gnashes his teeth, and becomes rigid. So I spoke to Your disciples, that they should cast it out, but they could not."

He answered him and said, "O faithless generation, how long shall I be with you? How long shall I bear with you? Bring him to Me."

Then they brought him to Him. And when he saw Him, immediately the spirit convulsed him, and he fell on the ground and wallowed, foaming at the mouth.

So He asked his father, "How long has this been happening to him?" And he said, "From childhood.

"And often he has thrown him both into the fire and into the water to destroy him. But if You can do anything, have compassion on us and help us."

Jesus said to him, "If you can believe, all things are possible to him who believes."

Immediately the father of the child cried out and said with tears, "Lord, I believe; help my unbelief!"

Mark 9:17–24

While He spoke these things to them, behold, a ruler came and worshiped Him, saying, "My daughter has just died, but come and lay Your hand on her and she will live."

So Jesus arose and followed him, and so did His disciples.

When Jesus came into the ruler's house, and saw the flute players and the noisy crowd wailing,

He said to them, "Make room, for the girl is not dead, but sleeping." And they ridiculed Him.

But when the crowd was put outside, He went in and took her by the hand, and the girl arose.

And the report of this went out into all that land.

Matthew 9:18–19, 23–26

Now when Jesus had entered Capernaum, a centurion came to Him, pleading with Him,

saying, "Lord, my servant is lying at home paralyzed, dreadfully tormented."

And Jesus said to him, "I will come and heal him."

The centurion answered and said, "Lord, I am not worthy that You should come under my roof. But only speak a word, and my servant will be healed.

"For I also am a man under authority, having soldiers under me. And I say to this one, 'Go,' and he goes; and to another, 'Come,' and he comes; and to my servant, 'Do this,' and he does it."

When Jesus heard it, He marveled, and said to those who followed, "Assuredly, I say to you, I have not found such great faith, not even in Israel!

"And I say to you that many will come from east and west, and sit down with Abraham, Isaac, and Jacob in the kingdom of heaven.

"But the sons of the kingdom will be cast out into outer darkness. There will be weeping and gnashing of teeth."

Then Jesus said to the centurion, "Go your way; and as you have believed, so let it be done for you." And his servant was healed that same hour.

Matthew 8:5–13

Then Nathan departed to his house. And the LORD struck the child that Uriah's wife bore to David, and it became ill.

David therefore pleaded with God for the child, and David fasted and went in and lay all night on the ground.

So the elders of his house arose and went to him, to raise him up from the ground. But he would not, nor did he eat food with them.

Then on the seventh day it came to pass that the child died. And the servants of David were afraid to tell him that the child was dead. For they said, "Indeed, while the child was alive, we spoke to him, and he would not heed our voice. How can we tell him that the child is dead? He may do some harm!"

When David saw that his servants were whispering, David perceived that the child was dead. Therefore David said to his servants, "Is the child dead?" And they said, "He is dead."

So David arose from the ground, washed and anointed himself, and changed his clothes; and he went into the house of the LORD and worshiped. Then he went to his own house; and when he requested, they set food before him, and he ate.

Then his servants said to him, "What is this that you have done? You fasted and wept for the child while he was alive, but when the child died, you arose and ate food."

And he said, "While the child was alive, I fasted and wept; for I said, 'Who can tell whether the LORD will be gracious to me, that the child may live?'

"But now he is dead; why should I fast? Can I bring him back again? I shall go to him, but he shall not return to me."

Then David comforted Bathsheba his wife, and went in to her and lay with her. So she bore a son, and he called his name Solomon. Now the LORD loved him.

II Samuel 12:15–24

Is anyone among you sick? Let him call for the elders of the church, and let them pray over him, anointing him with oil in the name of the Lord.

And the prayer of faith will save the sick, and the Lord will raise him up. And if he has committed sins, he will be forgiven.

Confess your trespasses to one another, and pray for one another, that you may be healed. The effective, fervent prayer of a righteous man avails much.

James 5:14–16

As one whom his mother comforts,
So I will comfort you;
And you shall be comforted in Jerusalem.

Isaiah 66:13

Your wife doesn't seem to understand you

∞

And the LORD God said, "It is not good that man should be alone; I will make him a helper comparable to him."

So Adam gave names to all cattle, to the birds of the air, and to every beast of the field. But for Adam there was not found a helper comparable to him.

And the LORD God caused a deep sleep to fall on Adam, and he slept; and He took one of his ribs, and closed up the flesh in its place.

Then the rib which the LORD God had taken from man He made into a woman, and He brought her to the man.

And Adam said:
"This is now bone of my bones
And flesh of my flesh;
She shall be called Woman,
Because she was taken out of Man."

Therefore a man shall leave his father and mother and be joined to his wife, and they shall become one flesh.

And they were both naked, the man and his wife, and were not ashamed.

Genesis 2:18, 20–25

Husbands, likewise, dwell with them with understanding, giving honor to the wife, as to the weaker vessel, and as being heirs together of the grace of life, that your prayers may not be hindered.

Finally, all of you be of one mind, having compassion for one another; love as brothers, be tenderhearted, be courteous;

not returning evil for evil or reviling for reviling, but on the contrary blessing, knowing that you were called to this, that you may inherit a blessing.

For

"He who would love life
And see good days,
Let him refrain his tongue from evil,
And his lips from speaking deceit.
Let him turn away from evil and do good;
Let him seek peace and pursue it."

I Peter 3:7–11

A word fitly spoken is like apples of gold
In settings of silver.

By long forbearance a ruler is persuaded,
And a gentle tongue breaks a bone.

Proverbs 25:11, 15

Though I speak with the tongues of men and of angels, but have not love, I have become sounding brass or a clanging cymbal.

And though I have the gift of prophecy, and understand all mysteries and all knowledge, and though I have all faith, so that I could remove mountains, but have not love, I am nothing.

And though I bestow all my goods to feed the poor, and though I give my body to be burned, but have not love, it profits me nothing.

Love suffers long and is kind; love does not envy; love does not parade itself, is not puffed up;

does not behave rudely, does not seek its own, is not provoked, thinks no evil; does not rejoice in iniquity, but rejoices in the truth;

Bears all things, believes all things, hopes all things, endures all things.

Love never fails. But whether there are prophecies, they will fail; whether there are tongues, they will cease; whether there is knowledge, it will vanish away.

For we know in part and we prophesy in part.

But when that which is perfect has come, then that which is in part will be done away.

When I was a child, I spoke as a child, I understood as a child, I thought as a child; but when I became a man, I put away childish things.

For now we see in a mirror, dimly, but then face to face. Now I know in part, but then I shall know just as I also am known.

And now abide faith, hope, love, these three; but the greatest of these is love.

I Corinthians 13:1–13

Let love be without hypocrisy. Abhor what is evil. Cling to what is good.

Be kindly affectionate to one another with brotherly love, in honor giving preference to one another.

Romans 12:9–10

Owe no one anything except to love one another, for he who loves another has fulfilled the law.

For the commandments, *"You shall not commit adultery," "You shall not murder," "You shall not steal," "You shall not bear false witness," "You shall not covet,"* and if there is any other commandment, are all summed up in this saying, namely, *"You shall love your neighbor as yourself."*

Love does no harm to a neighbor; therefore love is the fulfillment of the law.

Romans 13:8–10

Nevertheless, neither is man independent of woman, nor woman independent of man, in the Lord.

For as woman came from man, even so man also comes through woman; but all things are from God.

I Corinthians 11:11–12

For none of us lives to himself, and no one dies to himself.

Romans 14:7

Like a bird that wanders from its nest
Is a man who wanders from his place.

Proverbs 27:8

Two are better than one,
Because they have a good reward for their labor.
For if they fall, one will lift up his companion.
But woe to him who is alone when he falls,
For he has no one to help him up.
Again, if two lie down together, they will keep warm;
But how can one be warm alone?

Ecclesiastes 4:9–11

For if you love those who love you, what reward have you? Do not even the tax collectors do the same?

And if you greet your brethren only, what do you do more than others? Do not even the tax collectors do so?

Therefore you shall be perfect, just as your Father in heaven is perfect.

Matthew 5:46–48

You must discipline your children

∞

My son, do not despise the chastening of the LORD,
Nor detest His correction;
For whom the LORD loves He corrects,
Just as a father the son in whom he delights.

Proverbs 3:11–12

Furthermore, we have had human fathers who corrected us, and we paid them respect. Shall we not much more readily be in subjection to the Father of spirits and live?

For they indeed for a few days chastened us as seemed best to them, but He for our profit, that we may be partakers of His holiness.

Now no chastening seems to be joyful for the present, but painful; nevertheless, afterward it yields the peaceable fruit of righteousness to those who have been trained by it.

Hebrews 12:9–11

The rod and rebuke give wisdom,
But a child left to himself brings shame to his mother.

Correct your son, and he will give you rest;
Yes, he will give delight to your soul.

Proverbs 29:15, 17

Though He was a Son, yet He learned obedience by
the things which He suffered.

Hebrews 5:8

Now I rejoice, not that you were made sorry, but
that your sorrow led to repentance. For you were made
sorry in a godly manner, that you might suffer loss from
us in nothing.

II Corinthians 7:9

You shall beat him with a rod,
And deliver his soul from hell.

Proverbs 23:14

Chasten your son while there is hope,
And do not set your heart on his destruction.

Proverbs 19:18

Rebuke is more effective for a wise man
Than a hundred blows on a fool.

Proverbs 17:10

Hatred stirs up strife,
But love covers all sins.

Wisdom is found on the lips of him who has
understanding,
But a rod is for the back of him who is devoid of
understanding.

Proverbs 10:12–13

Whoever loves instruction loves knowledge,
But he who hates correction is stupid.
A good man obtains favor from the LORD,
But a man of wicked intentions He will condemn.
A man is not established by wickedness,
But the root of the righteous cannot be moved.

Proverbs 12:1–3

Consecrate yourselves therefore, and be holy, for I
am the LORD your God.

Leviticus 20:7

Therefore be very courageous to keep and to do all
that is written in the Book of the Law of Moses, lest you
turn aside from it to the right hand or to the left . . .

but you shall hold fast to the LORD your God, as
you have done to this day.

Joshua 23:6, 8

My son, keep my words,
And treasure my commands within you.

Keep my commands and live,
And my law as the apple of your eye.
Bind them on your fingers;
Write them on the tablet of your heart.

Proverbs 7:1–3

You feel powerless to shield your children from evils like drugs and alcohol

∞

Hear, O heavens, and give ear, O earth!
For the LORD has spoken:
"I have nourished and brought up children,
And they have rebelled against Me."

Isaiah 1:2

In the fear of the LORD there is strong confidence,
And His children will have a place of refuge.
The fear of the LORD is a fountain of life,
To turn one away from the snares of death.

Proverbs 14:26–27

Therefore hear me now, my children,
And do not depart from the words of my mouth.
Lest aliens be filled with your wealth,
And your labors go to the house of a foreigner;
And you mourn at last,
When your flesh and your body are consumed,
And say:
"How I have hated instruction,

And my heart despised correction!
I have not obeyed the voice of my teachers,
Nor inclined my ear to those who instructed me!
I was on the verge of total ruin,
In the midst of the assembly and congregation."

Proverbs 5:7, 10–14

In the way of righteousness is life,
And in its pathway there is no death.

Proverbs 12:28

Wine is a mocker,
Strong drink is a brawler,
And whoever is led astray by it is not wise.

Proverbs 20:1

A foolish son is a grief to his father,
And bitterness to her who bore him.

Proverbs 17:25

He who loves pleasure will be a poor man;
He who loves wine and oil will not be rich.

Proverbs 21:17

In mercy and truth
Atonement is provided for iniquity;
And by the fear of the LORD one departs from evil.

Proverbs 16:6

Take away the dross from silver,
And it will go to the silversmith for jewelry.

Proverbs 25:4

Do you not know that you are the temple of God and that the Spirit of God dwells in you?

If anyone defiles the temple of God, God will destroy him. For the temple of God is holy, which temple you are.

1 Corinthians 3:16–17

My son, if sinners entice you,
Do not consent.
So are the ways of everyone who is greedy for gain;
It takes away the life of its owners.

Proverbs 1:10, 19

And do not fear those who kill the body but cannot kill the soul. But rather fear Him who is able to destroy both soul and body in hell.

Matthew 10:28

For the law of the Spirit of life in Christ Jesus has made me free from the law of sin and death.

Romans 8:2

But whoever listens to me will dwell safely,
And will be secure, without fear of evil.

Proverbs 1:33

The merciful man does good for his own soul,
But he who is cruel troubles his own flesh.
Though they join forces, the wicked will not go unpunished;
But the posterity of the righteous will be delivered.

Proverbs 11:17, 21

My son, if you receive my words,
And treasure my commands within you,
So that you incline your ear to wisdom,
And apply your heart to understanding;
Yes, if you cry out for discernment,
And lift up your voice for understanding,
If you seek her as silver,
And search for her as for hidden treasures;
Then you will understand the fear of the LORD,
And find the knowledge of God.
For the LORD gives wisdom;
From His mouth come knowledge and understanding;
He stores up sound wisdom for the upright;
He is a shield to those who walk uprightly;
He guards the paths of justice,
And preserves the way of His saints.
Then you will understand righteousness and justice,
Equity and every good path.

Proverbs 2:1–9

GOD'S SPECIAL LOVE IS
WITH YOU WHEN

You bring your problems to Him

∞

For the LORD will not forsake His people, for His great name's sake, because it has pleased the LORD to make you His people.

I Samuel 12:22

Consider what I say, and may the Lord give you understanding in all things.
This is a faithful saying:
For if we died with Him,
We shall also live with Him.
If we endure,
We shall also reign with Him.
If we deny Him,
He also will deny us.

II Timothy 2:7, 11–12

The Spirit of the Lord GOD is upon Me,
Because the LORD has anointed Me
To preach good tidings to the poor;
He has sent Me to heal the brokenhearted,
To proclaim liberty to the captives,
And the opening of the prison to those who are bound;

To proclaim the acceptable year of the LORD,
And the day of vengeance of our God;
To comfort all who mourn,
To console those who mourn in Zion,
To give them beauty for ashes,
The oil of joy for mourning,
The garment of praise for the spirit of heaviness;
That they may be called trees of righteousness,
The planting of the LORD, that He may be glorified.

Isaiah 61:1–3

If you would prepare your heart,
And stretch out your hands toward Him;
If iniquity were in your hand, and you put it far
away,
And would not let wickedness dwell in your tents;
Then surely you could lift up your face without spot;
Yes, you could be steadfast, and not fear;
Because you would forget your misery,
And remember it as waters that have passed away,
And your life would be brighter than noonday.
Though you were dark, you would be like the
morning.
And you would be secure, because there is hope;
Yes, you would dig around you, and take your rest
in safety.

Job 11:13–18

Blessed be the LORD, who has given rest to His people Israel, according to all that He promised. There has not failed one word of all His good promise, which He promised through His servant Moses.

May the LORD our God be with us, as He was with our fathers. May He not leave us nor forsake us,

that He may incline our hearts to Himself, to walk in all His ways, and to keep His commandments and His statutes and His judgments, which He commanded our fathers.

And may these words of mine, with which I have made supplication before the LORD, be near the LORD our God day and night, that He may maintain the cause of His servant and the cause of His people Israel, as each day may require.

I Kings 8:56–59

"For the eyes of the LORD are on the righteous,
And His ears are open to their prayers;
But the face of the LORD is against those who do evil."

And who is he who will harm you if you become followers of what is good?

But even if you should suffer for righteousness' sake, you are blessed. *"And do not be afraid of their threats, nor be troubled."*

But sanctify the Lord God in your hearts, and always

be ready to give a defense to everyone who asks you a reason for the hope that is in you, with meekness and fear.

I Peter 3:12–15

We are hard-pressed on every side, yet not crushed; we are perplexed, but not in despair;

persecuted, but not forsaken; struck down, but not destroyed—

always carrying about in the body the dying of the Lord Jesus, that the life of Jesus also may be manifested in our body.

For all things are for your sakes, that grace, having spread through the many, may cause thanksgiving to abound to the glory of God.

Therefore we do not lose heart. Even though our outward man is perishing, yet the inward man is being renewed day by day.

For our light affliction, which is but for a moment, is working for us a far more exceeding and eternal weight of glory,

while we do not look at the things which are seen, but at the things which are not seen. For the things which are seen are temporary, but the things which are not seen are eternal.

II Corinthians 4:8–10, 15–18

And to give you who are troubled rest with us when the Lord Jesus is revealed from heaven with His mighty angels,

in flaming fire taking vengeance on those who do not know God, and on those who do not obey the gospel of our Lord Jesus Christ.

These shall be punished with everlasting destruction from the presence of the Lord and from the glory of His power,

when He comes, in that Day, to be glorified in His saints and to be admired among all those who believe, because our testimony among you was believed.

Therefore we also pray always for you that our God would count you worthy of this calling, and fulfill all the good pleasure of His goodness and the work of faith with power,

that the name of our Lord Jesus Christ may be glorified in you, and you in Him, according to the grace of our God and the Lord Jesus Christ.

II Thessalonians 1:7–12

Now thanks be to God who always leads us in triumph in Christ, and through us diffuses the fragrance of His knowledge in every place.

For we are to God the fragrance of Christ among those who are being saved and among those who are perishing.

To the one we are the aroma of death leading to death, and to the other the aroma of life leading to life. And who is sufficient for these things?

For we are not, as so many, peddling the word of God; but as of sincerity, but as from God, we speak in the sight of God in Christ.

II Corinthians 2:14–17

But Jesus looked at them and said to them, "With men this is impossible, but with God all things are possible."

Matthew 19:26

Yes, we had the sentence of death in ourselves, that we should not trust in ourselves but in God who raises the dead,

who delivered us from so great a death, and does deliver us; in whom we trust that He will still deliver us.

II Corinthians 1:9–10

You rely on Him to guide
and direct your children

∞

My little children, these things I write to you, so that you may not sin. And if anyone sins, we have an Advocate with the Father, Jesus Christ the righteous.

I John 2:1

For the Son of Man has come to seek and to save that which was lost.

Luke 19:10

Have you not known?
Have you not heard?
The everlasting God, the LORD,
The Creator of the ends of the earth,
Neither faints nor is weary.
His understanding is unsearchable.
He gives power to the weak,
And to those who have no might He increases strength.
Even the youths shall faint and be weary,
And the young men shall utterly fall,
But those who wait on the LORD
Shall renew their strength;

They shall mount up with wings like eagles,
They shall run and not be weary,
They shall walk and not faint.

Isaiah 40:28–31

He will guard the feet of His saints,
But the wicked shall be silent in darkness.
For by strength no man shall prevail.

I Samuel 2:9

I am a companion of all who fear You,
And of those who keep Your precepts.

Psalm 119:63

When you roam, they will lead you;
When you sleep, they will keep you;
And when you awake, they will speak with you.
For the commandment is a lamp,
And the law a light;
Reproofs of instruction are the way of life.

Proverbs 6:22–23

I, the LORD, have called You in righteousness,
And will hold Your hand;
I will keep You and give You as a covenant to the
people,
As a light to the Gentiles.

Isaiah 42:6

I will go before you
And make the crooked places straight;
I will break in pieces the gates of bronze
And cut the bars of iron.
I will give you the treasures of darkness
And hidden riches of secret places,
That you may know that I, the LORD,
Who call you by your name,
Am the God of Israel.

Isaiah 45:2–3

Do not remember the former things,
Nor consider the things of old.
Behold, I will do a new thing,
Now it shall spring forth;
Shall you not know it?
I will even make a road in the wilderness
And rivers in the desert.

Isaiah 43:18–19

Fear not, for I am with you;
Be not dismayed, for I am your God.
I will strengthen you,
Yes, I will help you,
I will uphold you with My righteous right hand.

Isaiah 41:10

"I have made the earth,
And created man on it.
I—My hands—stretched out the heavens,
And all their host I have commanded.
I have raised him up in righteousness,
And I will direct all his ways;
He shall build My city
And let My exiles go free,
Not for price nor reward,"
Says the LORD of hosts.

Isaiah 45:12–13

"For the mountains shall depart
And the hills be removed,
But My kindness shall not depart from you,
Nor shall My covenant of peace be removed,"
Says the LORD, who has mercy on you.

Isaiah 54:10

For as the rain comes down, and the snow from
heaven,
And do not return there,
But water the earth,
And make it bring forth and bud,
That it may give seed to the sower
And bread to the eater,
So shall My word be that goes forth from My mouth;

It shall not return to Me void,
But it shall accomplish what I please,
And it shall prosper in the thing for which I sent it.

Isaiah 55:10–11

A man's heart plans his way,
But the LORD directs his steps.

Proverbs 16:9

For we walk by faith, not by sight.

II Corinthians 5:7

You forgive your children
when they've done wrong
∞

He made known His ways to Moses,
His acts to the children of Israel.
The LORD is merciful and gracious,
Slow to anger, and abounding in mercy.
He will not always strive with us,
Nor will He keep His anger forever.
He has not dealt with us according to our sins,
Nor punished us according to our iniquities.
For as the heavens are high above the earth,
So great is His mercy toward those who fear Him;
As far as the east is from the west,
So far has He removed our transgressions from us.
As a father pities his children,
So the LORD pities those who fear Him.

Psalm 103:7–13

Then He said: "A certain man had two sons.

"And the younger of them said to *his* father, 'Father, give me the portion of goods that falls *to me*.' So he divided to them *his* livelihood.

"And not many days after, the younger son gathered

all together, journeyed to a far country, and there wasted his possessions with prodigal living.

"But when he had spent all, there arose a severe famine in that land, and he began to be in want.

"Then he went and joined himself to a citizen of that country, and he sent him into his fields to feed swine.

"And he would gladly have filled his stomach with the pods that the swine ate, and no one gave him anything.

"But when he came to himself, he said, 'How many of my father's hired servants have bread enough and to spare, and I perish with hunger!

"'I will arise and go to my father, and will say to him, "Father, I have sinned against heaven and before you,

"'"and I am no longer worthy to be called your son. Make me like one of your hired servants."'

"And he arose and came to his father. But when he was still a great way off, his father saw him and had compassion, and ran and fell on his neck and kissed him.

"And the son said to him, 'Father, I have sinned against heaven and in your sight, and am no longer worthy to be called your son.'

"But the father said to his servants, 'Bring out the best robe and put it on him, and put a ring on his hand and sandals on his feet.

"'And bring the fatted calf here and kill it, and let us eat and be merry;

"'for this my son was dead and is alive again; he was lost and is found.' And they began to be merry."

Luke 15:11–24

Then Peter came to Him and said, "Lord, how often shall my brother sin against me, and I forgive him? Up to seven times?"

Jesus said to him, "I do not say to you, up to seven times, but up to seventy times seven."

Matthew 18:21–22

You share your family's bounty with the poor

∞

He who has a generous eye will be blessed,
For he gives of his bread to the poor.

Proverbs 22:9

Listen, my beloved brethren: Has God not chosen the poor of this world to be rich in faith and heirs of the kingdom which He promised to those who love Him?

James 2:5

Jesus said to him, "If you want to be perfect, go, sell what you have and give to the poor, and you will have treasure in heaven; and come, follow Me."

But when the young man heard that saying, he went away sorrowful, for he had great possessions.

Then Jesus said to His disciples, "Assuredly, I say to you that it is hard for a rich man to enter the kingdom of heaven.

"And again I say to you, it is easier for a camel to go through the eye of a needle than for a rich man to enter the kingdom of God."

Matthew 19:21–24

What does it profit, my brethren, if someone says he has faith but does not have works? Can faith save him?

If a brother or sister is naked and destitute of daily food,

and one of you says to them, "Depart in peace, be warmed and filled," but you do not give them the things which are needed for the body, what does it profit?

Thus also faith by itself, if it does not have works, is dead.

James 2:14–17

You shall surely give to him, and your heart should not be grieved when you give to him, because for this thing the LORD your God will bless you in all your works and in all to which you put your hand.

For the poor will never cease from the land; therefore I command you, saying, "You shall open your hand wide to your brother, to your poor and your needy, in your land."

Deuteronomy 15:10–11

A poor man who oppresses the poor
Is like a driving rain which leaves no food.

Proverbs 28:3

He who oppresses the poor reproaches his Maker,
But he who honors Him has mercy on the needy.

Proverbs 14:31

The LORD makes poor and makes rich;
He brings low and lifts up.
He raises the poor from the dust
And lifts the beggar from the ash heap,
To set them among princes
And make them inherit the throne of glory.
"For the pillars of the earth are the LORD's,
And He has set the world upon them."

1 Samuel 2:7–8

He who mocks the poor reproaches his Maker;
He who is glad at calamity will not go unpunished.

Proverbs 17:5

Now the multitude of those who believed were of one heart and one soul; neither did anyone say that any of the things he possessed was his own, but they had all things in common.

And with great power the apostles gave witness to the resurrection of the Lord Jesus. And great grace was upon them all.

Nor was there anyone among them who lacked; for all who were possessors of lands or houses sold them, and brought the proceeds of the things that were sold,

and laid them at the apostles' feet; and they distributed to each as anyone had need.

Acts 4:32–35

Let the lowly brother glory in his exaltation,
but the rich in his humiliation, because as a flower
of the field he will pass away.

For no sooner has the sun risen with a burning heat
than it withers the grass; its flower falls, and its beautiful appearance perishes. So the rich man also will fade
away in his pursuits.

James 1:9–11

He who has a generous eye will be blessed,
For he gives of his bread to the poor.

Proverbs 22:9

You bring your family together in prayer

∞

For thus says the LORD:
"To the eunuchs who keep My Sabbaths,
And choose what pleases Me,
And hold fast My covenant,
Even to them I will give in My house
And within My walls a place and a name
Better than that of sons and daughters;
I will give them an everlasting name
That shall not be cut off.
Also the sons of the foreigner
Who join themselves to the LORD, to serve Him,
And to love the name of the LORD, to be His
servants—
Everyone who keeps from defiling the Sabbath,
And holds fast My covenant—
Even them I will bring to My holy mountain,
And make them joyful in My house of prayer.
Their burnt offerings and their sacrifices
Will be accepted on My altar;

For My house shall be called a house of prayer for all nations."

Isaiah 56:4–7

Delight yourself also in the LORD,
And He shall give you the desires of your heart.

Psalm 37:4

It shall come to pass
That before they call, I will answer;
And while they are still speaking, I will hear.

Isaiah 65:24

The LORD is near to all who call upon Him,
To all who call upon Him in truth.
He will fulfill the desire of those who fear Him;
He also will hear their cry and save them.

Psalm 145:18–19

Then I set my face toward the Lord God to make request by prayer and supplications, with fasting, sackcloth, and ashes.

And I prayed to the LORD my God, and made confession, and said, "O Lord, great and awesome God, who keeps His covenant and mercy with those who love Him, and with those who keep His commandments, "we have sinned and committed iniquity, we have done wickedly and rebelled, even by departing from Your precepts and Your judgments.

"Now therefore, our God, hear the prayer of Your servant, and his supplications, and for the Lord's sake cause Your face to shine on Your sanctuary, which is desolate.

"O my God, incline Your ear and hear; open Your eyes and see our desolations, and the city which is called by Your name; for we do not present our supplications before You because of our righteous deeds, but because of Your great mercies."

Daniel 9:3–5, 17–18

Call to Me, and I will answer you, and show you great and mighty things, which you do not know.

Jeremiah 33:3

You also helping together in prayer for us, that thanks may be given by many persons on our behalf for the gift granted to us through many.

For our boasting is this: the testimony of our conscience that we conducted ourselves in the world in simplicity and godly sincerity, not with fleshly wisdom but by the grace of God, and more abundantly toward you.

For we are not writing any other things to you than

what you read or understand. Now I trust you will understand, even to the end

(as also you have understood us in part), that we are your boast as you also are ours, in the day of the Lord Jesus.

II Corinthians 1:11–14

And whatever things you ask in prayer, believing, you will receive.

Matthew 21:22

Again I say to you that if two of you agree on earth concerning anything that they ask, it will be done for them by My Father in heaven.

For where two or three are gathered together in My name, I am there in the midst of them.

Matthew 18:19–20

I desire therefore that the men pray everywhere, lifting up holy hands, without wrath and doubting.

I Timothy 2:8

Let us therefore come boldly to the throne of grace, that we may obtain mercy and find grace to help in time of need.

Hebrews 4:16

And whatever we ask we receive from Him, because we keep His commandments and do those things that are pleasing in His sight.

I John 3:22

Rejoice in the Lord always. Again I will say, rejoice!

Let your gentleness be known to all men. The Lord is at hand.

Be anxious for nothing, but in everything by prayer and supplication, with thanksgiving, let your requests be made known to God;

and the peace of God, which surpasses all understanding, will guard your hearts and minds through Christ Jesus.

Philippians 4:4–7

GOD SHARES YOUR DREAMS FOR

Children who know His love and share it with others

∞

Therefore be imitators of God as dear children.

And walk in love, as Christ also has loved us and given Himself for us, an offering and a sacrifice to God for a sweet-smelling aroma.

Ephesians 5:1–2

Now the purpose of the commandment is love from a pure heart, from a good conscience, and from sincere faith.

I Timothy 1:5

And if you call on the Father, who without partiality judges according to each one's work, conduct yourselves throughout the time of your stay here in fear;

knowing that you were not redeemed with corruptible things, like silver or gold, from your aimless conduct received by tradition from your fathers,

but with the precious blood of Christ, as of a lamb without blemish and without spot.

He indeed was foreordained before the foundation of the world, but was manifest in these last times for you who through Him believe in God, who raised Him from the dead and gave Him glory, so that your faith and hope are in God.

Since you have purified your souls in obeying the truth through the Spirit in sincere love of the brethren, love one another fervently with a pure heart,

having been born again, not of corruptible seed but incorruptible, through the word of God which lives and abides forever.

I Peter 1:17–23

Again, a new commandment I write to you, which thing is true in Him and in you, because the darkness is passing away, and the true light is already shining.

He who says he is in the light, and hates his brother, is in darkness until now.

He who loves his brother abides in the light, and there is no cause for stumbling in him.

But he who hates his brother is in darkness and walks in darkness, and does not know where he is going, because the darkness has blinded his eyes.

I John 2:8–11

Now may our God and Father Himself, and our Lord Jesus Christ, direct our way to you.

And may the Lord make you increase and abound in love to one another and to all, just as we do to you.

I Thessalonians 3:11–12

But concerning brotherly love you have no need that I should write to you, for you yourselves are taught by God to love one another.

I Thessalonians 4:9

Therefore, as the elect of God, holy and beloved, put on tender mercies, kindness, humility, meekness, long-suffering;

bearing with one another, and forgiving one another, if anyone has a complaint against another; even as Christ forgave you, so you also must do.

But above all these things put on love, which is the bond of perfection.

Colossians 3:12–14

That Christ may dwell in your hearts through faith; that you, being rooted and grounded in love,

may be able to comprehend with all the saints what is the width and length and depth and height—

to know the love of Christ which passes knowledge; that you may be filled with all the fullness of God.

Now to Him who is able to do exceedingly abundantly above all that we ask or think, according to the power that works in us,

to Him be glory in the church by Christ Jesus to all generations, forever and ever. Amen.

Ephesians 3:17–21

We give thanks to the God and Father of our Lord Jesus Christ, praying always for you,

since we heard of your faith in Christ Jesus and of your love for all the saints.

Colossians 1:3–4

For you, brethren, have been called to liberty; only do not use liberty as an opportunity for the flesh, but through love serve one another.

For all the law is fulfilled in one word, even in this: *"You shall love your neighbor as yourself."*

Galatians 5:13–14

The fruit of the righteous is a tree of life,
And he who wins souls is wise.

Proverbs 11:30

And Jesus came and spoke to them, saying, "All authority has been given to Me in heaven and on earth.

"Go therefore and make disciples of all the nations, baptizing them in the name of the Father and of the Son and of the Holy Spirit,

"teaching them to observe all things that I have commanded you; and lo, I am with you always, even to the end of the age." Amen.

Matthew 28:18–20

And He said to them, "Go into all the world and preach the gospel to every creature."

Mark 16:15

A fruitful life for your family

∞

Praise the LORD!
Blessed is the man who fears the LORD,
Who delights greatly in His commandments.
His descendants will be mighty on earth;
The generation of the upright will be blessed.
Wealth and riches will be in his house,
And his righteousness endures forever.

Psalm 112:1–3

I will rejoice in Jerusalem,
And joy in My people;
The voice of weeping shall no longer be heard in her,
Nor the voice of crying.
No more shall an infant from there live but a
few days,
Nor an old man who has not fulfilled his days;
For the child shall die one hundred years old,
But the sinner being one hundred years old shall
be accursed.
They shall build houses and inhabit them;
They shall plant vineyards and eat their fruit.
They shall not build and another inhabit;

They shall not plant and another eat;
For as the days of a tree, so shall be the days of My people,
And My elect shall long enjoy the work of their hands.
They shall not labor in vain,
Nor bring forth children for trouble;
For they shall be the descendants of the blessed of the LORD,
And their offspring with them.
It shall come to pass
That before they call, I will answer;
And while they are still speaking, I will hear.

Isaiah 65:19–24

That our sons may be as plants grown up in their youth;
That our daughters may be as pillars,
Sculptured in palace style;
That our barns may be full,
Supplying all kinds of produce;
That our sheep may bring forth thousands
And ten thousands in our fields;
That our oxen may be well laden;
That there be no breaking in or going out;
That there be no outcry in our streets.

Happy are the people who are in such a state;
Happy are the people whose God is the LORD!

Psalm 144:12–15

The wicked covet the catch of evil men,
But the root of the righteous yields fruit.
The wicked is ensnared by the transgression of
his lips,
But the righteous will come through trouble.
A man will be satisfied with good by the fruit of his
mouth,
And the recompense of a man's hands will be
rendered to him.

Proverbs 12:12–14

For God will save Zion
And build the cities of Judah,
That they may dwell there and possess it.
Also, the descendants of His servants shall inherit it,
And those who love His name shall dwell in it.

Psalm 69:35–36

For the LORD God is a sun and shield;
The LORD will give grace and glory;
No good thing will He withhold
From those who walk uprightly.

O LORD of hosts,
Blessed is the man who trusts in You!

Psalm 84:11–12

Let Your work appear to Your servants,
And Your glory to their children.
And let the beauty of the LORD our God be upon us,
And establish the work of our hands for us;
Yes, establish the work of our hands.

Psalm 90:16–17

Behold, I will bring them from the north country,
And gather them from the ends of the earth,
Among them the blind and the lame,
The woman with child
And the one who labors with child, together;
A great throng shall return there.
They shall come with weeping,
And with supplications I will lead them.
I will cause them to walk by the rivers of waters,
In a straight way in which they shall not stumble;
For I am a Father to Israel,
And Ephraim is My firstborn.
Hear the word of the LORD, O nations,
And declare it in the isles afar off, and say,
"He who scattered Israel will gather him,
And keep him as a shepherd does his flock."

Jeremiah 31:8–10

"No more shall every man teach his neighbor, and every man his brother, saying, 'Know the LORD,' for they all shall know Me, from the least of them to the greatest of them," says the LORD. "For I will forgive their iniquity, and their sin I will remember no more."

Jeremiah 31:34

The house of the wicked will be overthrown,
But the tent of the upright will flourish.

Proverbs 14:11

"In that day I will make a covenant for them
With the beasts of the field,
With the birds of the air,
And with the creeping things of the ground.
Bow and sword of battle I will shatter from the earth,
To make them lie down safely.
I will betroth you to Me forever;
Yes, I will betroth you to Me
In righteousness and justice,
In lovingkindness and mercy;
I will betroth you to Me in faithfulness,
And you shall know the LORD.
It shall come to pass in that day
That I will answer," says the LORD;
"I will answer the heavens,

And they shall answer the earth.
The earth shall answer
With grain,
With new wine,
And with oil;
They shall answer Jezreel.
Then I will sow her for Myself in the earth,
And I will have mercy on her who had not
obtained mercy;
Then I will say to those who were not My people,
'You are My people!'
And they shall say, 'You are my God!'"

Hosea 2:18–23

A peaceful and more hopeful world
for your children

All the ends of the world
Shall remember and turn to the LORD,
And all the families of the nations
Shall worship before You.
For the kingdom is the LORD's,
And He rules over the nations.
All the prosperous of the earth
Shall eat and worship;
All those who go down to the dust
Shall bow before Him,
Even he who cannot keep himself alive.
A posterity shall serve Him.
It will be recounted of the Lord to the next
generation,
They will come and declare His righteousness to a
people who will be born,
That He has done this.

Psalm 22:27–31

If it is possible, as much as depends on you, live
peaceably with all men.

Beloved, do not avenge yourselves, but rather give place to wrath; for it is written, *"Vengeance is Mine, I will repay,"* says the Lord.

Therefore
"If your enemy is hungry, feed him;
If he is thirsty, give him a drink;
For in so doing you will heap coals of fire on his head."

Do not be overcome by evil, but overcome evil with good.

Romans 12:18–21

When a man's ways please the LORD,
He makes even his enemies to be at peace with him.

Proverbs 16:7

The mountains will bring peace to the people,
And the little hills, by righteousness.
He will bring justice to the poor of the people;
He will save the children of the needy,
And will break in pieces the oppressor.
They shall fear You
As long as the sun and moon endure,
Throughout all generations.
He shall come down like rain upon the grass before mowing,
Like showers that water the earth.
In His days the righteous shall flourish,
And abundance of peace,

Until the moon is no more.
He shall have dominion also from sea to sea,
And from the River to the ends of the earth.
Those who dwell in the wilderness will bow before Him,
And His enemies will lick the dust.

Psalm 72:3–9

Surely His salvation is near to those who fear Him,
That glory may dwell in our land.
Mercy and truth have met together;
Righteousness and peace have kissed.
Truth shall spring out of the earth,
And righteousness shall look down from heaven.
Yes, the LORD will give what is good;
And our land will yield its increase.
Righteousness will go before Him,
And shall make His footsteps our pathway.

Psalm 85:9–13

For yet a little while and the wicked shall be no more;
Indeed, you will look carefully for his place,
But it shall be no more.
But the meek shall inherit the earth,
And shall delight themselves in the abundance of peace.

The wicked plots against the just,
And gnashes at him with his teeth.
The Lord laughs at him,
For He sees that his day is coming.

Psalm 37:10–13

Oh, give thanks to the LORD, for He is good!
For His mercy endures forever.
Let the redeemed of the LORD say so,
Whom He has redeemed from the hand of the enemy,
And gathered out of the lands,
From the east and from the west,
From the north and from the south.
They wandered in the wilderness in a desolate way;
They found no city to dwell in.
Hungry and thirsty,
Their soul fainted in them.
Then they cried out to the LORD in their trouble,
And He delivered them out of their distresses.
And He led them forth by the right way,
That they might go to a city for a dwelling place.
Oh, that men would give thanks to the LORD for
His goodness,
And for His wonderful works to the children of men!
For He satisfies the longing soul,
And fills the hungry soul with goodness.

Psalm 107:1–9

GOD REJOICES
WHEN

Your family anticipates
His return

∞

Behold what manner of love the Father has bestowed on us, that we should be called children of God! Therefore the world does not know us, because it did not know Him.

Beloved, now we are children of God; and it has not yet been revealed what we shall be, but we know that when He is revealed, we shall be like Him, for we shall see Him as He is.

And everyone who has this hope in Him purifies himself, just as He is pure.

I John 3:1–3

For behold, I create new heavens and a new earth;
And the former shall not be remembered or come to mind.
But be glad and rejoice forever in what I create;
For behold, I create Jerusalem as a rejoicing,
And her people a joy.
I will rejoice in Jerusalem,
And joy in My people;

The voice of weeping shall no longer be heard in her,
Nor the voice of crying.

Isaiah 65:17–19

So the ransomed of the LORD shall return,
And come to Zion with singing,
With everlasting joy on their heads.
They shall obtain joy and gladness;
Sorrow and sighing shall flee away.

Isaiah 51:11

To such as keep His covenant,
And to those who remember
His commandments to do them.
The LORD has established His throne in heaven,
And His kingdom rules over all.

Psalm 103:18–19

It is good that one should hope and wait quietly
For the salvation of the LORD.

Lamentations 3:26

For as the lightning comes from the east and flashes
to the west, so also will the coming of the Son of
Man be.

For wherever the carcass is, there the eagles will be
gathered together.

Immediately after the tribulation of those days the sun will be darkened, and the moon will not give its light; the stars will fall from heaven, and the powers of the heavens will be shaken.

Then the sign of the Son of Man will appear in heaven, and then all the tribes of the earth will mourn, and they will see the Son of Man coming on the clouds of heaven with power and great glory.

And He will send His angels with a great sound of a trumpet, and they will gather together His elect from the four winds, from one end of heaven to the other.

Matthew 24:27–31

And there will be signs in the sun, in the moon, and in the stars; and on the earth distress of nations, with perplexity, the sea and the waves roaring;

men's hearts failing them from fear and the expectation of those things which are coming on the earth, for the powers of the heavens will be shaken.

Then they will see the Son of Man coming in a cloud with power and great glory.

Now when these things begin to happen, look up and lift up your heads, because your redemption draws near.

Luke 21:25–28

But the day of the Lord will come as a thief in the night, in which the heavens will pass away with a great noise, and the elements will melt with fervent heat; both the earth and the works that are in it will be burned up.

Therefore, since all these things will be dissolved, what manner of persons ought you to be in holy conduct and godliness,

looking for and hastening the coming of the day of God, because of which the heavens will be dissolved, being on fire, and the elements will melt with fervent heat?

II Peter 3:10–12

He who believes in the Son of God has the witness in himself; he who does not believe God has made Him a liar, because he has not believed the testimony that God has given of His Son.

And this is the testimony: that God has given us eternal life, and this life is in His Son.

He who has the Son has life; he who does not have the Son of God does not have life.

These things I have written to you who believe in the name of the Son of God, that you may know that you have eternal life, and that you may continue to believe in the name of the Son of God.

I John 5:10–13

Who also said, "Men of Galilee, why do you stand gazing up into heaven? This same Jesus, who was taken up from you into heaven, will so come in like manner as you saw Him go into heaven."

Acts 1:11

And God will wipe away every tear from their eyes; there shall be no more death, nor sorrow, nor crying. There shall be no more pain, for the former things have passed away.

Revelation 21:4

Looking for the blessed hope and glorious appearing of our great God and Savior Jesus Christ.

Titus 2:13

You dedicate your children to Him

∞

Their descendants shall be known among the
Gentiles,
And their offspring among the people.
All who see them shall acknowledge them,
That they are the posterity whom the LORD has
blessed.
I will greatly rejoice in the LORD,
My soul shall be joyful in my God;
For He has clothed me with the garments of
salvation,
He has covered me with the robe of righteousness,
As a bridegroom decks himself with ornaments,
And as a bride adorns herself with her jewels.
For as the earth brings forth its bud,
As the garden causes the things that are sown in it to
spring forth,
So the Lord GOD will cause righteousness and praise
to spring forth before all the nations.

Isaiah 61:9–11

For as many of you as were baptized into Christ have put on Christ.

There is neither Jew nor Greek, there is neither slave nor free, there is neither male nor female; for you are all one in Christ Jesus.

And if you are Christ's, then you are Abraham's seed, and heirs according to the promise.

Galatians 3:27–29

And when eight days were completed for the circumcision of the Child, His name was called JESUS, the name given by the angel before He was conceived in the womb.

Now when the days of her purification according to the law of Moses were completed, they brought Him to Jerusalem to present Him to the Lord

(as it is written in the law of the Lord, *"Every male who opens the womb shall be called holy to the LORD"*),

and to offer a sacrifice according to what is said in the law of the Lord, *"A pair of turtledoves or two young pigeons."*

Luke 2:21–24

For I will pour water on him who is thirsty,
And floods on the dry ground;
I will pour My Spirit on your descendants,
And My blessing on your offspring.

Isaiah 44:3

Who has performed and done it,
Calling the generations from the beginning?
"I, the LORD, am the first;
And with the last I am He."

Isaiah 41:4

But now, O LORD,
You are our Father;
We are the clay, and You our potter;
And all we are the work of Your hand.

Isaiah 64:8

And she was in bitterness of soul, and prayed to the LORD and wept in anguish.

Then she made a vow and said, "O LORD of hosts, if You will indeed look on the affliction of Your maidservant and remember me, and not forget Your maidservant, but will give Your maidservant a male child, then I will give him to the LORD all the days of his life, and no razor shall come upon his head."

So it came to pass in the process of time that Hannah conceived and bore a son, and called his name Samuel, saying, "Because I have asked for him from the LORD."

Now the man Elkanah and all his house went up to offer to the LORD the yearly sacrifice and his vow.

But Hannah did not go up, for she said to her

husband, "Not until the child is weaned; then I will take him, that he may appear before the LORD and remain there forever."

So Elkanah her husband said to her, "Do what seems best to you; wait until you have weaned him. Only let the LORD establish His word." Then the woman stayed and nursed her son until she had weaned him.

And she said, "O my lord! As your soul lives, my lord, I am the woman who stood by you here, praying to the LORD.

"For this child I prayed, and the LORD has granted me my petition which I asked of Him.

"Therefore I also have lent him to the LORD; as long as he lives he shall be lent to the LORD." So they worshiped the LORD there.

I Samuel 1:10–11, 20–23, 26–28

But Samuel ministered before the LORD, even as a child, wearing a linen ephod.

Moreover his mother used to make him a little robe, and bring it to him year by year when she came up with her husband to offer the yearly sacrifice.

And Eli would bless Elkanah and his wife, and say, "The LORD give you descendants from this woman for the loan that was given to the LORD." Then they would go to their own home.

I Samuel 2:18–20

And now, little children, abide in Him, that when He appears, we may have confidence and not be ashamed before Him at His coming.

I John 2:28

A little one shall become a thousand,
And a small one a strong nation.
I, the LORD, will hasten it in its time.

Isaiah 60:22

You trust Him and wait for His answers

∞

I waited patiently for the LORD;
And He inclined to me,
And heard my cry.

Psalm 40:1

My soul, wait silently for God alone,
For my expectation is from Him.
He only is my rock and my salvation;
He is my defense;
I shall not be moved.
In God is my salvation and my glory;
The rock of my strength,
And my refuge, is in God.
Trust in Him at all times, you people;
Pour out your heart before Him;
God is a refuge for us. Selah

Psalm 62:5–8

Let all those who hate Zion
Be put to shame and turned back.
Let them be as the grass on the housetops,

Which withers before it grows up,
With which the reaper does not fill his hand,
Nor he who binds sheaves, his arms.
Neither let those who pass by them say,
"The blessing of the LORD be upon you;
We bless you in the name of the LORD!"

Psalm 129:5–8

Turn back, my daughters, go—for I am too old to have a husband. If I should say I have hope, if I should have a husband tonight and should also bear sons,

would you wait for them till they were grown? Would you restrain yourselves from having husbands? No, my daughters; for it grieves me very much for your sakes that the hand of the LORD has gone out against me!"

But Ruth said:

"Entreat me not to leave you,
Or to turn back from following after you;
For wherever you go, I will go;
And wherever you lodge, I will lodge;
Your people shall be my people,
And your God, my God.
Where you die, I will die,
And there will I be buried.
The LORD do so to me, and more also,
If anything but death parts you and me."

When she saw that she was determined to go with her, she stopped speaking to her.

So Boaz took Ruth and she became his wife; and when he went in to her, the LORD gave her conception, and she bore a son.

Then the women said to Naomi, "Blessed be the LORD, who has not left you this day without a close relative; and may his name be famous in Israel!

"And may he be to you a restorer of life and a nourisher of your old age; for your daughter-in-law, who loves you, who is better to you than seven sons, has borne him."

Then Naomi took the child and laid him on her bosom, and became a nurse to him.

Also the neighbor women gave him a name, saying, "There is a son born to Naomi." And they called his name Obed. He is the father of Jesse, the father of David.

Ruth 1:12–13, 16–18; 4:13–17

Every word of God is pure;
He is a shield to those who put their trust in Him.
Proverbs 30:5

But those who wait on the LORD
Shall renew their strength;
They shall mount up with wings like eagles,

They shall run and not be weary,
They shall walk and not faint.

Isaiah 40:31

I am the LORD, and there is no other;
There is no God besides Me.
I will gird you, though you have not known Me,
That they may know from the rising of the sun to its setting
That there is none besides Me.
I am the LORD, and there is no other.

Isaiah 45:5–6

For since the beginning of the world
Men have not heard nor perceived by the ear,
Nor has the eye seen any God besides You,
Who acts for the one who waits for Him.

Isaiah 64:4

You shall eat in plenty and be satisfied,
And praise the name of the LORD your God,
Who has dealt wondrously with you;
And My people shall never be put to shame.

Joel 2:26

The LORD your God in your midst,
The Mighty One, will save;

He will rejoice over you with gladness,
He will quiet you with His love,
He will rejoice over you with singing.

Zephaniah 3:17

That you do not become sluggish, but imitate those who through faith and patience inherit the promises.

Hebrews 6:12

As unknown, and yet well known; as dying, and behold we live; as chastened, and yet not killed;

as sorrowful, yet always rejoicing; as poor, yet making many rich; as having nothing, and yet possessing all things.

II Corinthians 6:9–10

For assuredly, I say to you, till heaven and earth pass away, one jot or one tittle will by no means pass from the law till all is fulfilled.

Whoever therefore breaks one of the least of these commandments, and teaches men so, shall be called least in the kingdom of heaven; but whoever does and teaches them, he shall be called great in the kingdom of heaven.

For I say to you, that unless your righteousness exceeds the righteousness of the scribes and Pharisees, you will by no means enter the kingdom of heaven.

Matthew 5:18–20

Do not be deceived, my beloved brethren.

Every good gift and every perfect gift is from above, and comes down from the Father of lights, with whom there is no variation or shadow of turning.

James 1:16–17

Jesus Christ is the same yesterday, today, and forever.

Hebrews 13:8

You teach your children
to show mercy to others

∞

And all his sons and all his daughters arose to comfort him.

Genesis 37:35a

Therefore the LORD has recompensed me
according to my righteousness,
According to my cleanness in His eyes.
With the merciful You will show Yourself merciful;
With a blameless man You will show Yourself
blameless.

II Samuel 22:25–26

If you extend your soul to the hungry
And satisfy the afflicted soul,
Then your light shall dawn in the darkness,
And your darkness shall be as the noonday.
The LORD will guide you continually,
And satisfy your soul in drought,
And strengthen your bones;
You shall be like a watered garden,
And like a spring of water, whose waters do not fail.

Those from among you
Shall build the old waste places;
You shall raise up the foundations of many
generations;
And you shall be called the Repairer of the Breach,
The Restorer of Streets to Dwell In.

Isaiah 58:10–12

But love your enemies, do good, and lend, hoping
for nothing in return; and your reward will be great, and
you will be sons of the Most High. For He is kind to the
unthankful and evil.

Therefore be merciful, just as your Father also is
merciful.

Judge not, and you shall not be judged. Condemn
not, and you shall not be condemned. Forgive, and you
will be forgiven.

Give, and it will be given to you: good measure,
pressed down, shaken together, and running over will be
put into your bosom. For with the same measure that
you use, it will be measured back to you.

Luke 6:35–38

And let us not grow weary while doing good, for in
due season we shall reap if we do not lose heart.

Therefore, as we have opportunity, let us do good to
all, especially to those who are of the household of faith.

Galatians 6:9–10

When her neighbors and relatives heard how the Lord had shown great mercy to her, they rejoiced with her.

Luke 1:58

Bear one another's burdens, and so fulfill the law of Christ.

Galatians 6:2

GOD'S DYNAMIC EXAMPLES OF FATHERS WHO CARED

Abraham

∞

Now the LORD had said to Abram:
"Get out of your country,
From your family
And from your father's house,
To a land that I will show you.
I will make you a great nation;
I will bless you
And make your name great;
And you shall be a blessing.
I will bless those who bless you,
And I will curse him who curses you;
And in you all the families of the earth shall be blessed."

Genesis 12:1–3

And the LORD said to Abram, after Lot had separated from him: "Lift your eyes now and look from the place where you are—northward, southward, eastward, and westward;

"for all the land which you see I give to you and your descendants forever.

"And I will make your descendants as the dust of

the earth; so that if a man could number the dust of the earth, then your descendants also could be numbered."

Genesis 13:14–16

After these things the word of the LORD came to Abram in a vision, saying, "Do not be afraid, Abram. I am your shield, your exceedingly great reward."

But Abram said, "Lord GOD, what will You give me, seeing I go childless, and the heir of my house is Eliezer of Damascus?"

Then Abram said, "Look, You have given me no offspring; indeed one born in my house is my heir!"

And behold, the word of the LORD came to him, saying, "This one shall not be your heir, but one who will come from your own body shall be your heir."

Then He brought him outside and said, "Look now toward heaven, and count the stars if you are able to number them." And He said to him, "So shall your descendants be."

And he believed in the LORD, and He accounted it to him for righteousness.

Genesis 15:1–6

When Abram was ninety-nine years old, the LORD appeared to Abram and said to him, "I am Almighty God; walk before Me and be blameless.

"And I will make My covenant between Me and you, and will multiply you exceedingly."

Then Abram fell on his face, and God talked with him, saying:

"As for Me, behold, My covenant is with you, and you shall be a father of many nations.

"No longer shall your name be called Abram, but your name shall be Abraham; for I have made you a father of many nations."

Genesis 17:1–5

For it is written that Abraham had two sons: the one by a bondwoman, the other by a freewoman.

But he who was of the bondwoman was born according to the flesh, and he of the freewoman through promise,

which things are symbolic. For these are the two covenants: the one from Mount Sinai which gives birth to bondage, which is Hagar.

Galatians 4:22–24

And Jesus said to him, "Today salvation has come to this house, because he also is a son of Abraham."

Luke 19:9

He opened the rock, and water gushed out;
It ran in the dry places like a river.

For He remembered His holy promise,
And Abraham His servant.
He brought out His people with joy,
His chosen ones with gladness.
He gave them the lands of the Gentiles,
And they inherited the labor of the nations,
That they might observe His statutes
And keep His laws.
Praise the LORD!

Psalm 105:41–45

Therefore know that only those who are of faith are sons of Abraham.

And the Scripture, foreseeing that God would justify the Gentiles by faith, preached the gospel to Abraham beforehand, saying, "In you all the nations shall be blessed."

So then those who are of faith are blessed with believing Abraham.

Galatians 3:7–9

And the LORD visited Sarah as He had said, and the LORD did for Sarah as He had spoken.

For Sarah conceived and bore Abraham a son in his old age, at the set time of which God had spoken to him.

And Abraham called the name of his son who was born to him—whom Sarah bore to him—Isaac.

Then Abraham circumcised his son Isaac when he was eight days old, as God had commanded him.

Now Abraham was one hundred years old when his son Isaac was born to him.

And Sarah said, "God has made me laugh, and all who hear will laugh with me."

She also said, "Who would have said to Abraham that Sarah would nurse children? For I have borne him a son in his old age."

So the child grew and was weaned. And Abraham made a great feast on the same day that Isaac was weaned.

Genesis 21:1–8

Jacob

∞

Sing aloud to God our strength;
Make a joyful shout to the God of Jacob.
Raise a song and strike the timbrel,
The pleasant harp with the lute.
Blow the trumpet at the time of the New Moon,
At the full moon, on our solemn feast day.
For this is a statute for Israel,
A law of the God of Jacob.

Psalm 81:1–4

I am the LORD your God,
Who brought you out of the land of Egypt;
Open your mouth wide, and I will fill it.

Psalm 81:10

Then the Lord awoke as from sleep,
Like a mighty man who shouts because of wine.
And He beat back His enemies;
He put them to a perpetual reproach.
Moreover He rejected the tent of Joseph,
And did not choose the tribe of Ephraim,
But chose the tribe of Judah,

Mount Zion which He loved.
And He built His sanctuary like the heights,
Like the earth which He has established forever.
He also chose David His servant,
And took him from the sheepfolds;
From following the ewes that had young He brought
him,
To shepherd Jacob His people,
And Israel His inheritance.
So he shepherded them according to the integrity
of his heart,
And guided them by the skillfulness of his hands.

Psalm 78:65–72

Then Jacob was left alone; and a Man wrestled with him until the breaking of day.

Now when He saw that He did not prevail against him, He touched the socket of his hip; and the socket of Jacob's hip was out of joint as He wrestled with him.

And He said, "Let Me go, for the day breaks." But he said, "I will not let You go unless You bless me!"

So He said to him, "What is your name?" He said, "Jacob."

And He said, "Your name shall no longer be called Jacob, but Israel; for you have struggled with God and with men, and have prevailed."

Then Jacob asked, saying, "Tell me Your name, I

pray." And He said, "Why is it that you ask about My name?" And He blessed him there.

So Jacob called the name of the place Peniel: "For I have seen God face to face, and my life is preserved."

Genesis 32:24–30

Then God said to Jacob, "Arise, go up to Bethel and dwell there; and make an altar there to God, who appeared to you when you fled from the face of Esau your brother."

And Jacob said to his household and to all who were with him, "Put away the foreign gods that are among you, purify yourselves, and change your garments.

"Then let us arise and go up to Bethel; and I will make an altar there to God, who answered me in the day of my distress and has been with me in the way which I have gone."

Genesis 35:1–3

And God said to him, "Your name is Jacob; your name shall not be called Jacob anymore, but Israel shall be your name." So He called his name Israel.

Also God said to him: "I am God Almighty. Be fruitful and multiply; a nation and a company of nations shall proceed from you, and kings shall come from your body."

Genesis 35:10–11

Then they sent the tunic of many colors, and they brought it to their father and said, "We have found this. Do you know whether it is your son's tunic or not?"

And he recognized it and said, "It is my son's tunic. A wild beast has devoured him. Without doubt Joseph is torn to pieces."

Then Jacob tore his clothes, put sackcloth on his waist, and mourned for his son many days.

And all his sons and all his daughters arose to comfort him; but he refused to be comforted, and he said, "For I shall go down into the grave to my son in mourning." Thus his father wept for him.

Genesis 37:32–35

When Jacob saw that there was grain in Egypt, Jacob said to his sons, "Why do you look at one another?"

And he said, "Indeed I have heard that there is grain in Egypt; go down to that place and buy for us there, that we may live and not die."

Genesis 42:1–2

But when they told him all the words which Joseph had said to them, and when he saw the carts which Joseph had sent to carry him, the spirit of Jacob their father revived.

Then Israel said, "It is enough. Joseph my son is still alive. I will go and see him before I die."

Genesis 45:27–28

Joseph—Jacob's son
∞

And to Joseph were born two sons before the years of famine came, whom Asenath, the daughter of Poti-Pherah priest of On, bore to him.

Joseph called the name of the firstborn Manasseh: "For God has made me forget all my toil and all my father's house."

And the name of the second he called Ephraim: "For God has caused me to be fruitful in the land of my affliction."

Then the seven years of plenty which were in the land of Egypt ended,

and the seven years of famine began to come, as Joseph had said. The famine was in all lands, but in all the land of Egypt there was bread.

So when all the land of Egypt was famished, the people cried to Pharaoh for bread. Then Pharaoh said to all the Egyptians, "Go to Joseph; whatever he says to you, do."

The famine was over all the face of the earth, and Joseph opened all the storehouses and sold to the Egyptians. And the famine became severe in the land of Egypt.

So all countries came to Joseph in Egypt to buy grain, because the famine was severe in all lands.

Genesis 41:50–57

Then Joseph could not restrain himself before all those who stood by him, and he cried out, "Make everyone go out from me!" So no one stood with him while Joseph made himself known to his brothers.

And he wept aloud, and the Egyptians and the house of Pharaoh heard it.

Then Joseph said to his brothers, "I am Joseph; does my father still live?" But his brothers could not answer him, for they were dismayed in his presence.

And Joseph said to his brothers, "Please come near to me." So they came near. Then he said: "I am Joseph your brother, whom you sold into Egypt.

"But now, do not therefore be grieved or angry with yourselves because you sold me here; for God sent me before you to preserve life.

"For these two years the famine has been in the land, and there are still five years in which there will be neither plowing nor harvesting.

"And God sent me before you to preserve a posterity for you in the earth, and to save your lives by a great deliverance.

"So now it was not you who sent me here, but God; and He has made me a father to Pharaoh, and lord of all his house, and a ruler throughout all the land of Egypt.

"Hurry and go up to my father, and say to him, 'Thus says your son Joseph: "God has made me lord of all Egypt; come down to me, do not tarry.

"'"You shall dwell in the land of Goshen, and you shall be near to me, you and your children, your children's children, your flocks and your herds, and all that you have."'"

Genesis 45:1–10

Then Joseph provided his father, his brothers, and all his father's household with bread, according to the number in their families.

Genesis 47:12

Then Israel saw Joseph's sons, and said, "Who are these?"

Joseph said to his father, "They are my sons, whom God has given me in this place." And he said, "Please bring them to me, and I will bless them."

Now the eyes of Israel were dim with age, so that he could not see. Then Joseph brought them near him, and he kissed them and embraced them.

Genesis 48:8–10

Then Joseph fell on his father's face and wept over him, and kissed him.

Genesis 50:1

David

∞

Arise, O LORD, to Your resting place,
You and the ark of Your strength.
Let Your priests be clothed with righteousness,
And let Your saints shout for joy.
For Your servant David's sake,
Do not turn away the face of Your Anointed.
The LORD has sworn in truth to David;
He will not turn from it:
"I will set upon your throne the fruit of your body.
If your sons will keep My covenant
And My testimony which I shall teach them,
Their sons also shall sit upon your throne
forevermore."
For the LORD has chosen Zion;
He has desired it for His dwelling place:
"This is My resting place forever;
Here I will dwell, for I have desired it.
I will abundantly bless her provision;
I will satisfy her poor with bread.
I will also clothe her priests with salvation,
And her saints shall shout aloud for joy.
There I will make the horn of David grow;

I will prepare a lamp for My Anointed.
His enemies I will clothe with shame,
But upon Himself His crown shall flourish."

Psalm 132:8–18

Incline your ear, and come to Me.
Hear, and your soul shall live;
And I will make an everlasting covenant with you—
The sure mercies of David.
Indeed I have given him as a witness to the people,
A leader and commander for the people.

Isaiah 55:3–4

Then David spoke to the LORD the words of this song, on the day when the LORD had delivered him from the hand of all his enemies, and from the hand of Saul.

"For You are my lamp, O LORD;
The LORD shall enlighten my darkness.
For by You I can run against a troop;
By my God I can leap over a wall.
As for God, His way is perfect;
The word of the LORD is proven;
He is a shield to all who trust in Him.
For who is God, except the LORD?
And who is a rock, except our God?
God is my strength and power,
And He makes my way perfect.

He makes my feet like the feet of deer,
And sets me on my high places.
He teaches my hands to make war,
So that my arms can bend a bow of bronze.
You have also given me the shield of Your salvation;
Your gentleness has made me great."

II Samuel 22:1, 29–36

For David says concerning Him:
"I foresaw the LORD always before my face,
For He is at my right hand, that I may not be shaken."

Acts 2:25

Just as David also describes the blessedness of the man to whom God imputes righteousness apart from works:
"Blessed are those whose lawless deeds are forgiven,
And whose sins are covered;
Blessed is the man to whom the LORD shall not
impute sin."

Romans 4:6–8

And David said to his son Solomon, "Be strong and of good courage, and do it; do not fear nor be dismayed, for the LORD God—my God—will be with you. He will not leave you nor forsake you, until you have finished all the work for the service of the house of the LORD."

I Chronicles 28:20

As for you, if you walk before Me as your father David walked, and do according to all that I have commanded you, and if you keep My statutes and My judgments,

then I will establish the throne of your kingdom, as I covenanted with David your father, saying, "You shall not fail to have a man as ruler in Israel."

II Chronicles 7:17–18

Manoah—Samson's father

∞

Again the children of Israel did evil in the sight of the LORD, and the LORD delivered them into the hand of the Philistines for forty years.

Now there was a certain man from Zorah, of the family of the Danites, whose name was Manoah; and his wife was barren and had no children.

And the Angel of the LORD appeared to the woman and said to her, "Indeed now, you are barren and have borne no children, but you shall conceive and bear a son.

"Now therefore, please be careful not to drink wine or similar drink, and not to eat anything unclean.

"For behold, you shall conceive and bear a son. And no razor shall come upon his head, for the child shall be a Nazirite to God from the womb; and he shall begin to deliver Israel out of the hand of the Philistines."

So the woman came and told her husband, saying, "A Man of God came to me, and His countenance was like the countenance of the Angel of God, very awesome; but I did not ask Him where He was from, and He did not tell me His name.

"And He said to me, 'Behold, you shall conceive

and bear a son. Now drink no wine or similar drink, nor eat anything unclean, for the child shall be a Nazirite to God from the womb to the day of his death.'"

Judges 13:1–7

So the woman bore a son and called his name Samson; and the child grew, and the LORD blessed him.

And the Spirit of the LORD began to move upon him at Mahaneh Dan between Zorah and Eshtaol.

Judges 13:24–25

Zacharias—John's father

∞

There was in the days of Herod, the king of Judea, a certain priest named Zacharias, of the division of Abijah. His wife was of the daughters of Aaron, and her name was Elizabeth.

And they were both righteous before God, walking in all the commandments and ordinances of the Lord blameless.

But they had no child, because Elizabeth was barren, and they were both well advanced in years.

So it was, that while he was serving as priest before God in the order of his division,

according to the custom of the priesthood, his lot fell to burn incense when he went into the temple of the Lord.

And the whole multitude of the people was praying outside at the hour of incense.

Then an angel of the Lord appeared to him, standing on the right side of the altar of incense.

And when Zacharias saw him, he was troubled, and fear fell upon him.

But the angel said to him, "Do not be afraid,

Zacharias, for your prayer is heard; and your wife Elizabeth will bear you a son, and you shall call his name John.

"And you will have joy and gladness, and many will rejoice at his birth.

"For he will be great in the sight of the Lord, and shall drink neither wine nor strong drink. He will also be filled with the Holy Spirit, even from his mother's womb."

Luke 1:5–15

Now Elizabeth's full time came for her to be delivered, and she brought forth a son.

When her neighbors and relatives heard how the Lord had shown great mercy to her, they rejoiced with her.

So it was, on the eighth day, that they came to circumcise the child; and they would have called him by the name of his father, Zacharias.

His mother answered and said, "No; he shall be called John."

But they said to her, "There is no one among your relatives who is called by this name."

So they made signs to his father—what he would have him called.

And he asked for a writing tablet, and wrote, saying, "His name is John." So they all marveled.

Immediately his mouth was opened and his tongue loosed, and he spoke, praising God.

Now his father Zacharias was filled with the Holy Spirit, and prophesied, saying:

"Blessed is the Lord God of Israel,

For He has visited and redeemed His people . . ."

So the child grew and became strong in spirit, and was in the deserts till the day of his manifestation to Israel.

Luke 1:57–64, 67–68, 80

Noah
∞

And he called his name Noah, saying, "This one will comfort us concerning our work and the toil of our hands, because of the ground which the LORD has cursed."

Genesis 5:29

So the LORD said, "I will destroy man whom I have created from the face of the earth, both man and beast, creeping thing and birds of the air, for I am sorry that I have made them."

But Noah found grace in the eyes of the LORD.

This is the genealogy of Noah. Noah was a just man, perfect in his generations. Noah walked with God.

And Noah begot three sons: Shem, Ham, and Japheth.

Genesis 6:7–10

Then the LORD said to Noah, "Come into the ark, you and all your household, because I have seen that you are righteous before Me in this generation."

So Noah, with his sons, his wife, and his sons' wives, went into the ark because of the waters of the flood.

Genesis 7:1, 7

So He destroyed all living things which were on the face of the ground: both man and cattle, creeping thing and bird of the air. They were destroyed from the earth. Only Noah and those who were with him in the ark remained alive.

And the waters prevailed on the earth one hundred and fifty days.

Then God remembered Noah, and every living thing, and all the animals that were with him in the ark. And God made a wind to pass over the earth, and the waters subsided.

Genesis 7:23–8:1

Then God spoke to Noah, saying,

"Go out of the ark, you and your wife, and your sons and your sons' wives with you."

Genesis 8:15–16

So God blessed Noah and his sons, and said to them: "Be fruitful and multiply, and fill the earth."

Then God spoke to Noah and to his sons with him, saying:

"And as for Me, behold, I establish My covenant with you and with your descendants after you."

Genesis 9:1, 8–9

But without faith it is impossible to please Him, for he who comes to God must believe that He is, and that He is a rewarder of those who diligently seek Him.

By faith Noah, being divinely warned of things not yet seen, moved with godly fear, prepared an ark for the saving of his household, by which he condemned the world and became heir of the righteousness which is according to faith.

Hebrews 11:6–7

Joseph, Mary's husband

∞

Now the birth of Jesus Christ was as follows: After His mother Mary was betrothed to Joseph, before they came together, she was found with child of the Holy Spirit.

Then Joseph her husband, being a just man, and not wanting to make her a public example, was minded to put her away secretly.

But while he thought about these things, behold, an angel of the Lord appeared to him in a dream, saying, "Joseph, son of David, do not be afraid to take to you Mary your wife, for that which is conceived in her is of the Holy Spirit.

"And she will bring forth a Son, and you shall call His name JESUS, for He will save His people from their sins."

So all this was done that it might be fulfilled which was spoken by the Lord through the prophet, saying:

"Behold, the virgin shall be with child, and bear a Son, and they shall call His name Immanuel," which is translated, "God with us."

Then Joseph, being aroused from sleep, did as the angel of the Lord commanded him and took to him his wife, and did not know her till she had brought forth her firstborn Son. And he called His name Jesus.

Matthew 1:18–25

Now when they had departed, behold, an angel of the Lord appeared to Joseph in a dream, saying, "Arise, take the young Child and His mother, flee to Egypt, and stay there until I bring you word; for Herod will seek the young Child to destroy Him."

When he arose, he took the young Child and His mother by night and departed for Egypt . . .

Now when Herod was dead, behold, an angel of the Lord appeared in a dream to Joseph in Egypt,

saying, "Arise, take the young Child and His mother, and go to the land of Israel, for those who sought the young Child's life are dead."

Then he arose, took the young Child and His mother, and came into the land of Israel.

Matthew 2:13–14, 19–21

SPECIAL BIRTHDAYS

My Children _____

_____

_____

_____

_____

_____

_____

_____

_____

_____

_____

_____

_____

_____

_____

_____

_____

_____

_____

_____

_____

SPECIAL BIRTHDAYS

My Grandchildren _____

_____

_____

_____

_____

_____

_____

_____

_____

_____

_____

_____

_____

_____

_____

_____

_____

_____

_____

_____

_____

_____

_____

SPECIAL BIRTHDAYS

Other _____

_____

_____

_____

_____

_____

_____

_____

_____

_____

_____

_____

_____

_____

_____

_____

_____

_____

_____

_____

_____

FATHER'S PRAYER NOTES

FATHER'S PRAYER NOTES

_____
_____
_____
_____
_____
_____
_____
_____
_____
_____
_____
_____
_____
_____
_____
_____
_____
_____
_____
_____
_____
_____
_____